From Boy Soldier to Major
British Army 1931-72

by

Major Frederick Lloyd Price MBE

Edited by Malcolm K. Johnson

Grosvenor House
Publishing Limited

This book is published by
Grosvenor House Publishing Ltd
Link House
140 The Broadway, Tolworth, Surrey, KT6 7HT.
www.grosvenorhousepublishing.co.uk

A CIP record for this book
is available from the British Library

ISBN 978-1-83975-489-0

THIS BOOK IS DEDICATED TO THE MEMORY OF THE OFFICERS, NON-COMMISSIONED OFFICERS AND MEN WHO SERVED WITH THE 2ND BATTALION KING'S OWN YORKSHIRE LIGHT INFANTRY DURING WORLD WAR TWO. ESPECIALLY THOSE WHO HAVE NO KNOWN GRAVES

COVERING NOTE OF RECOLLECTIONS DOCUMENT

The following document was written by FLP over an extensive time, 35+ years and intermittently; hence there was some repetition of statements and terminology. It was also typed on his old typewriter, which inevitably gave typing errors because of its keyboard and his deteriorating vision from glaucoma.

I have retyped the document into a Word programme, as it was written, apart from the following....

a) Spelling and typo corrections.
b) Correction of place name spellings.
c) Adjustment of date reference, ie he refers to Chaubattia 1932 as 50 years ago whereas it is now 80 years.
d) Additional insert for clarification of Indian currency; Rupee, Annas, Paisa, Pies.
e) Added distances, altitudes of various locations where he left them blank.
f) I have split the document into sections covering his life up to retirement in 1972, namely..

    1) Family and Boyhood, Yorkshire.
    2) Enlistment aged 14 yrs, 1931 - 1945 KOYLI.
    3) Post War, RASC 1945 - 1963.

4) Reorganisation RASC to RAOC 1963 - 1972.

And further added...

- A listing of his medals.
- A map showing his/KOYLI movements through India, Burma and Siam.
- A Glossary of terms, not commonly used.

There are numerous photographs covering the above and a listing of these is further attached with reference numbers.

Ian Leslie Price (son)

Contents

FORWORD

This is a remarkable story of a lifetime spent in the British Army. There can be very few ex-soldiers who joined the British Army at the age of fourteen and began their military service in India which, at the time, was one of the most important outposts of the British Empire. Joining the army at the age of fourteen is also quite unusual, although in the eighteenth century one of the countries greatest generals, Sir John Moore, joined the 51st Regiment of Foot at the age of fifteen. The 51st Regiment of Foot eventually became the King's Own Yorkshire Light Infantry and on August 1st 1759 the Regiment took part in the battle of Minden, near Hanover in northern Germany, in which they distinguished themselves when, together with five other regiments it helped to drive off a French cavalry charge with the power of its musket fire. After the battle the men picked white roses found growing on the battlefield and wore them in their hats, a tradition that was carried on by the regiment every 1st August and resulted in that date becoming Yorkshire Day. The Regiment also took part in the Battle of Waterloo, fought near the Belgium village of Braine-l'Alleud on 18 June 1815, but then spent most of the nineteenth century in India, the North West Frontier and Burma. During the 1881 Army reforms the 51st was paired with 105th Madras European Light Infantry, which eventually brought about the 1st and 2nd Battalions of the King's Own Yorkshire Light Infantry. In 1927 King George V honoured the regiment when he appointed Her Majesty - the late Queen Mother, then Duchess of York, the Regiment's Colonel in Chief. Her Majesty was delighted and remained a proud and faithful friend of the King's Own Yorkshire Light Infantry for the remainder of her life.

Today, a boy wishing to join the British Army has to be 16 years or over and have the consent of his parents; once he reaches the age of 18 years he can make the decision for himself. Both Sir John Moore, and Major Frederick Lloyd Price, the main character in this more modern story, were assigned to the 2nd Battalion King's Own Yorkshire Light Infantry. Colonel Tim Collins, a veteran of the Iraq War maintains that if the recruiting of today's young people were to be stopped it would destroy the opportunities for many of those from disadvantaged backgrounds. The reader is free to agree or disagree on this point when they have followed the story of Major Price.

At the end of 1921, 2nd KOYLI returned to England from service in Ireland and on 6th March of that year the Battalion sailed for India and the Far East where it was destined to remain until after the Second World War. Towards the end of 1949, 2nd KOYLI had seen some twenty-eight years service in the Far East of the British Empire.

Volume Five of the Regimental History entitled, *Never Give Up*, was compiled by Major J.R. Dugmore and published in 1950. This history deals with the period 1919-1942, and Chapter eight is entitled *Tragedy in Burma*. The accounts of the fighting in Burma were gathered from a number of men who had similar experiences to those Major Price endured. On a number of occasions Major Price makes critical comments of the Regimental History's record of events and, while he may be correct in asserting what took place in his small group, there were many similar groups dotted around the same area which would have had different experiences.

Throughout history many veterans of conflicts have written accounts of the events in which they were involved. The nature of military conflict can often be such that accounts by two of the participants can often be quite different. Before publishing his war memoirs of the same Burma campaign, during which he experienced the same conditions as Major Price, Captain R.E.S. Tanner, also of 2nd KOYLI, volunteered himself for a study of his memory by the Department of Experimental Psychology at the University of Oxford. The main conclusions of this study were that, 'We do not know the physical and much less the mental conditions of the soldiers in this Battalion in 1942, but we can assume that there was a progressive deterioration in what they were able to see, hear and remember afterwards; fear and food shortages would have ensured it. Memories of warfare have to be judiciously interpreted with as much triangulation as is available from any historical resource.' *BURMA 1942: MEMORIES OF A RETREAT, R.E.S. Tanner and D.A. Tanner, The History Press, 2009. p.45.*

The Burma Campaign was, from the British point of view, one of the most tragic episodes of the Second World War. The physical conditions in which it was fought placed a huge strain on all those involved. The complete disregard by both sides for the basic, and generally accepted, rules of warfare has placed this episode of the Second World War somewhat apart from the experience of those who fought in Europe and North Africa. Unfortunately, it would seem that those who fought in the Far East during World War II have not received the degree of attention, understanding and appreciation that has been so generously, and quite rightly, extended to those who fought in the European and North African campaigns.

Malcolm K. Johnson

Acknowledgements

There are a number of people, mainly members of the Price family, who have contributed to the preservation of this soldier's story. The family of Major Price are to be congratulated in that, not only have they preserved this former soldier's story, but have also made the effort to bring it to a wider audience. During the twentieth century the British Army was involved in two world wars which changed the lives of those involved. After the Second World War numerous major and minor conflicts, in many parts of the world, continued to change the prospects or those involved. While the British Army has not always been as successful as it would have wished, its care and concern for its young soldiers has not had a great deal of publicity. The telling of this story should go some way towards rectifying this aspect of life in the British Army.

The basic story of Major Price's early life, followed by his career in the British Army, is told by Major Price himself, a feat that few could manage with such detail and clarity. Major Price spent a great deal of his service in India and Burma and there are few accounts of the conditions and the type of warfare that took place there before and during the Second World War. This story should go some way towards understanding, and sympathising with, those who fought and died in this campaign in what was generally called 'The Far East'.

Special thanks must go to his son, Ian Leslie Price, who gathered the information from his father's notes, that were retrieved by Nicola Hicks (The daughter of Major Price's niece), which rendered the task of editing that much easier.

Malcolm K. Johnson

Major Frederick Price MBE

1. Member of the British Empire (Military)
2. 39-45 Star.
3. Burma Star.
4. Defence Medal.
5. 39-45 War Medal.
6. General Service Medal.
7. Long Service & Good Conduct Medal (Army).
8. Army Meritorious Service Medal.
9. Pingat Jasa Malaysia Medal.

Listed by Frederick Michael Price (son)

Chapter Headings

MAP OF INDIA, BURMA, SIAM WITH LINES FOR ROUTE

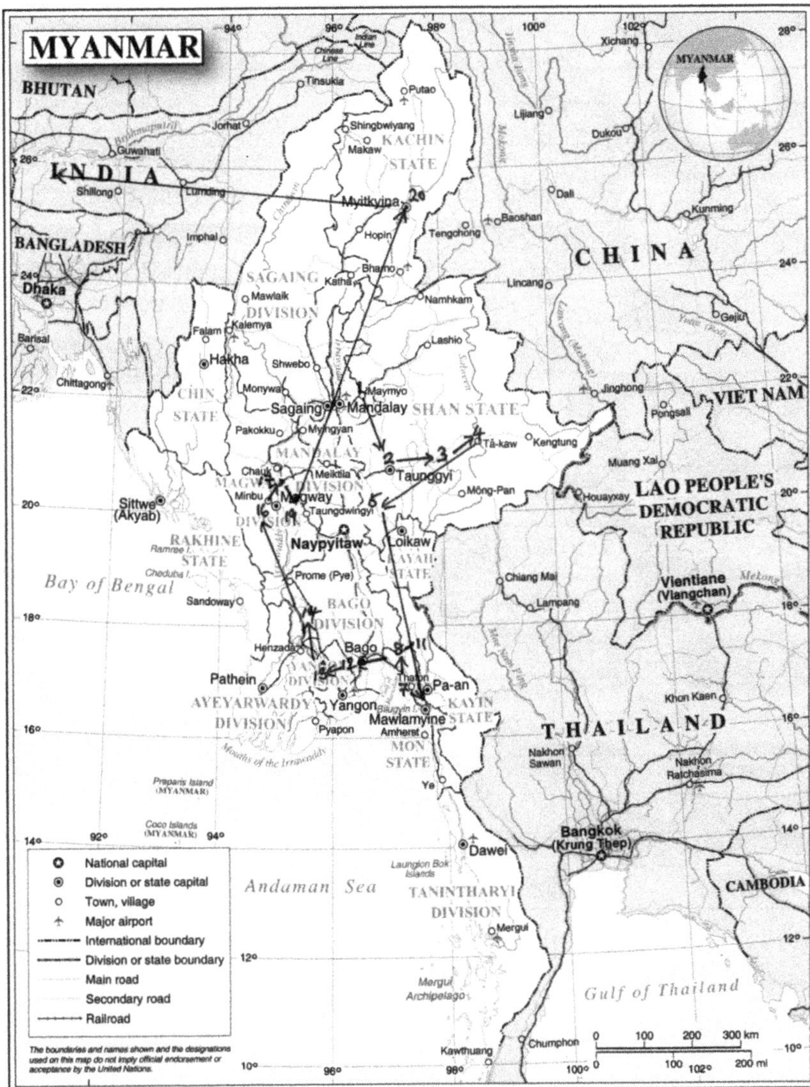

Map No. 4168 Rev. 3 UNITED NATIONS
June 2012

Department of Field Support
Cartographic Section

ROUTE OF RETREAT THROUGH BURMA

#	LOCATION	MAP REFERENCE	DISTANCE (CROW)	APPROX. DATE	MODE
1	MAYMYO	22 02N, 96 27E		23 AUG 1941	
			95M 152KM		?
2	TAUNGGYI	20 47N, 97 02E		DEC 1941	
			85M 136KM		?
3	LOI LAM	22 38N, 98 81E		DEC 1941	
			130M 209KM		?
4	TA KAW	21 13N, 98 42E		DEC 1941	
			20M 32KM		FOOT
5	KALAW	20 38N, 96 34E		JAN 1942	
			20M 32KM		TRAIN
6	HAINALE	?			
			241M 389KM		TRAIN
7	THATON	16 56N, 97 22E		02 FEB 1942	
			22M 35KM		FOOT
8	BILIN	17 14N, 97 15E		12 FEB 1942	
			220M 354KM		ROAD/ FOOT
9	DANYINGON	17 16N, 97 14E		16 FEB 1942	

			211M 339KM		FOOT
10	KYAIKTO	17 18N, 97 01E		21 FEB 1942	
			211M 339KM		FOOT
11	MOKPALIN/	17 26 N, 96 53E			
	SITTANG		208M 334KM		
12	PEGU	17 20N, 96 28E			
			23M 37KM		FOOT/ TRAIN
13	HLEGU	17 14N, 96 14E			
			48M 77KM		FOOT
14	THARRAWADDY	17 39N, 95 48E			
			39M 62KM		FOOT
15	HMAWBI	17 06N, 96 03E			
			220M 354KM		FOOT
16	MAGWE	20 09N, 94 57E			
			21M 35KM		FOOT
17	YENANGYAUNG	20 27N, 94 52E			
			106M 172KM		FOOT
18	THITYAGAUK	19 58N, 95 16E			

			?		FOOT/ TANK
19	TOKSAN	20 01N, 95 03E			
			355M 570KM		AT CART/ TRAIN
20	MYITYINA	25 23N, 97 24E			
					PLANE
21	ASSAM, INDIA				

FAMILY LIFE AND BOYHOOD IN YORKSHIRE

I was born in Barn Cottages in the village of Stillingfleet on 23rd February 1917, the eighth son of a family of nine sons, and was christened in St Helen's Church about two hundred yards from where I was born. At this time a family of nine was not unusual, but being all of the same sex was a little out of the ordinary and must have been a great disappointment to my mother. Barn Cottages are still standing today but with considerable modification.

My mother's father, grandfather and great-grandfather were all born, married and buried in Stillingfleet. My grandfather, William Spencer, born in 1847, also had nine children. My great-grandfather, George Spencer, born in 1813, had six children. My great-great-grandfather, Henry, born in 1790 had ten children. My great-great-great-grandfather Edward, born in 1749, had twelve children, which shows to some extent that we were a vigorous lot by any standard. Stillingfleet is mentioned in the "Domesday" book as "Steflingflet", "Flet" being the name of the "Beck" or stream that flows through the centre of the village before connecting with the river Ouse. Stillingfleet, a small village based largely on agriculture, is situated on the eastern bank of the River Ouse, some seven miles south of York. When the river is in spate the overflow runs off into the Beck and and when I was a boy visiting my grandmother in Stillingfleet, and coming from Kelfield, this often happened and I had to make a detour around the village because the wooden bridge over the Beck was under water. The village boasts a Church, Post Office, Public House and until recently, a School. The adjacent villages of Kelfield and Moreby, and until 1850 Acaster Selby, are in the parish of Stillingfleet which had a population of 418 in 1841, but only 352 in 1891.

The majority of marriages up to the early twentieth century were residents of the parish or nearby villages. There being no transport, other than the horse, walking was the norm. It would be no exaggeration to say that the great majority of the villagers of Stillingfleet at this period were blood related to me. My father was born in Great Horwood, Buckinghamshire in 1881 and came to Yorkshire in his late teens on a government work scheme. The scheme guaranteed him work for at least a year and he was employed as a farm labourer in Acaster Malbis where he met my mother who was working on Cundall's Farm as a maid, or skivvy as they were then known which was also in Acaster Malbis. They were married in the Parish Church in 1902. My wife Sheleagh and I visited Acaster Malbis in 1973, soon after my retirement from the army. After making a number of enquiries in the village, we obtained the key to the church from an elderly and frail Miss Cundall, a onetime warden of the church. She was the daughter of the late barrister farmer Cundall and the last of the family line. She was happy to show us around the church, which had many plaques and tombstones relating to the Cundall family. I made a copy of my parent's marriage certificate which was signed by my mother and father and witnessed by my uncle Robert and aunt Zillah. After an extremely interesting and detailed tour of this very small and beautiful church, Miss Cundall invited us back to the farm for tea. It was no longer a working farm, but a secluded residence for herself and an elderly retainer, who was dressed in black with a small white apron and a white lace headband. The long drive leading to the farm was unkempt and dilapidated with lots of pot-holes and weeds. Unpainted stable doors hung off their hinges, the rose garden was a mass of elongated rose bushes and an unpainted boathouse stood at the bottom of the garden on the bank of the river Ouse. We had tea from a silver teapot and dainty cucumber sandwiches from a silver cake stand. We were shown a large number of photographs and silhouettes but none of my mother. The sitting room where we had tea was finished in prim Victorian style and was extremely clean and tidy but very over furnished with beautiful framed pictures, antiques and furniture. In its heyday this erstwhile gentleman's farm must have been a prosperous, tidy and well maintained establishment, with a considerable number of employees. Here was I, sitting in a room, which my mother as a very young girl must have cleaned and drinking tea from a silver teapot which she had probably polished well over eighty years ago. It put me into a somewhat pensive and meditative mood and closer to my mother than I had ever been. We thanked Miss Cundall for her hospitality and for a very interesting and informative day.

In 1902, when my parents married, all farm workers lived in "tied cottages" owned by their employer. This meant that every time they changed their place of employment they had to change their house. The farm year commenced and finished on "Lady Day", 25th March. It was later changed to the "Martinmass Day" (or Michaelmass), 11th November. Those requiring work, gathered in the market place, or other suitable meeting places, where they were questioned and inspected by their future employer as to their physical fitness, experience and previous place of work. I saw this procedure taking place in 1930, in the market place in Selby and got the impression that the farmer considered he was buying a farm animal and not a human being. This made a lasting impression on me, confirming my decision not to go to work on a farm, as all my brothers had done on leaving school, but to join the army. The going rate for a fourteen year old boy on leaving school and working twelve hours a day on a farm for six and a half days a week was £12 a year, plus food and lodging. Contracts were agreed by shaking hands and the acceptance by the employee of one shilling. As a result of this general annual movement of my family, my eldest brother William was born in Acaster Malbis, the next three, Charles, Henry and James, were born in Warthill and the next four, the twins Albert & Thomas, Sidney and myself were born in Stillingfleet. The next and last, David, was born in Kelfield.

We moved to Kelfield on the 14th February, when I was just under two years of age. The sparse family possessions, beds, chairs, tin bath, tin trunks, tables, pots and pans and a few other oddments, were loaded onto a horse drawn trully, loaned to my father by his new employer, Mr Knowland Hare of Kelfield Grange. I understand that I was the only one that rode on the truly, the rest of the family walked, my father leading the horse. I have no recollection of living in our first residence in Kelfield because we only stayed there for about three months until another promised larger house was available. The three months temporary arrangement must have been awful for my parents and family. It consisted of eight various sized houses in the Yard or Square in the centre of the village. The number of inhabitants was approximately thirty nine of which twenty eight were children. There was a purpose built pigeon cote - not in use, a twin seated midden, (a primitive type of earthen toilet) for thirty nine people and one water pump for fresh water. My parents must have been very pleased and relieved when they moved out and had their own individual toilet and water pump. Today, it is just impossible to visualise how the people managed to exist in such awful crowded and terribly unsanitary conditions. In 1947, the whole Yard/Square was condemned as being unfit for human habitation and was demolished and, standing in its place today is just one bungalow.

We moved into our second home, the centre cottages of three, across the road from the 'Yard' and next to the chapel. We had our own toilet and water supply - pump, which was an enormous improvement for the whole family. On one side was a family of nine by the name of Golton, and on the other side an elderly family, the Bells with a grown up daughter who was slightly retarded. Mr Bell was a retired farm worker when I was about ten years of age. I remember him telling me that he had worked on the same farm for over fifty years and, showing me with considerable pride the pocket watch he had been given on his retirement. To me it looked a very small reward for fifty years of hard and strenuous work in all weathers. His daughter Nellie went to the Grey Horse Inn every Saturday night with a jug for the family beer.

Our house had two bedrooms and two rooms downstairs. The smaller of the two bedrooms was occupied by my parents and the baby, David. The other bedroom was quite large and accommodated the rest of the family together with two double sized beds and two or three tin trunks. We were seldom at full strength because, between the ages of twelve and fourteen, you fled the nest and found employment on a farm as a 'living-in worker'. The two rooms downstairs were a front room for living, dining and cooking, the second room, very small, had a wash basin and small table. Furniture in the front room was sparse because of the limited space. A dining table was positioned in the centre of the room, under which everyone dumped their boots when going to bed. Two small chairs and a horsehair sofa were near the wall and a rocking chair at each end of the fireplace for mother and father. There was an open fire with oven and a fire heated boiler with a capacity of about a gallon. The mantelpiece had an elaborate woven coloured cloth surround, plus a string for hanging wet socks, tea-towels etc. There were several iron hooks above the fire grate for hanging cooking pots, pans and the kettle and the oven and the open fire were the sole means for all cooking. The brass fender in front of the fire, together with a brass poker, shovel and tongs, were religiously polished and the fireplace black-leaded. Pricked cloth rugs covered the rough and uneven red brick floor. A door in the corner of the room led to the stairs and the bedrooms. All our meals were taken in the front room and except for my parents we all stood up to eat; the only way to get access to the table.

The soil toilet was about fifteen yards away from the house and was of the midden type, having a trapdoor at the rear to enable the contents to be raked out when it got too piled up for comfort. The raked out soil formed a midden several feet from the trapdoor and muck from the pigsty was added to it. Periodically, generally in spring time, it was moved in a wheelbarrow to the garden. Strangely, I cannot ever remember being aware of the smell or the prevalence of flies; I probably considered it so normal and natural at the time. The majority of families in the village kept pigs and had the same sanitary procedures. Adjoining the toilet was an outhouse containing a coal store, wood store, wash-house with copper boiler, straw store and pigsty - which probably offset the smell from the toilet. The garden was about one acre in size and provided all our requirements in respect of vegetables and fruit, plus barley and straw for the pigs. The barley was cut by hand using a scythe and after being stoked for several days to dry, was taken to the farm for milling on a Saturday afternoon. The farmer charged a fee for this service.

Kelfield is a small rural village on the north bank of the river Ouse and a mile or so from the main road to York and Selby. In the 1920's there were about eighty-three residences, the majority being tied cottages. Agriculture was the main means of employment. Kelfield was part of the parish of Stillingfleet and had a population in the 1920's of 282, although one hundred years earlier the population had been 309. The village had a small Post Office, a school with about sixty pupils, all between the ages of four and fourteen, a chapel, a shop and a public house - The Grey Horse. One person, Mr A. Hare, with an assistant, carried out the work of wheelwright, carpenter, joiner, undertaker and blacksmith. A police constable based in Riccall, an adjoining village, periodically patrolled the village. Except for the poaching of rabbits and pheasants, which was considered to be a very serious crime and carried a prison sentence, plus the probability of losing one's employment and residence, at this time there was little for the police to do. There was no real vandalism and children involved in mischief were reported by the constable to the parents who administered the necessary chastisement. The constable's word was rarely questioned. Occasionally a villager was summoned for riding a bicycle after dark without a light, but these were rare events. There was no running water, gas or electricity in the village and no street lighting of any kind. Candles and paraffin lamps were the only means of providing light after darkness fell. In winter, except on festive occasions, the great majority of villagers were in bed and the houses in complete darkness by 9 pm. With the exception of the odd farmhouse, there were no bathrooms in any of the houses. A tin bath, which normally hung on a nail on the rear wall of the house, sufficed. It was brought into the house and placed in front of the fire, generally once a week on a Saturday night.

Several farmers moved their cows through the village from the grazing grounds to the farm for milking twice a day, leaving a long and dirty trail of cow dung. It was rarely swept up as this would have been a complete waste of time as fresh droppings occurred daily. A large number of horse drawn vehicles passed through the village but in their case the droppings were quickly gathered up for use on gardens. Almost every household in the village kept a pig or two. When a pig was killed, neighbours, friends and the person killing the pig, were given and expected a generous amount of 'bits and pieces'. Children put a bid in for the bladder weeks prior to the killing of the pig, and before the bladder was barely cold, with bits of fat sticking to it, it was blown up using a bicycle pump and used as a football. It was quite unpleasant when it hit you in the face, which I remember happening on many occasions. The bladder would last for about a week before it became hard and brittle and eventually burst. The 'playing field' was the main road. When a bladder, which was considered a luxury, was not available, a rubber ball or tin can was used. All children, especially boys, wore hob-nailed boots.

I remember my father killing a pig when I was about five years of age. A rope was put through the ring in the pig's nose and then threaded through the handle of the back door. When the rope was pulled tight, the pig's head was firmly held against the door. The 'coup de grace' was then delivered using a humane killer, an ugly looking weapon something like an axe with a spike opposite the blade. It took two blows to kill the pig and its shriek of pain could be heard all over the village. Its throat was then cut and the blood carefully collected to make black puddings. The carcase was then placed in a wooden tub and boiling water poured over it to facilitate the scraping off of the bristles. When all the innards had been removed, the carcase was hung in the woodshed for several days and then cut up and salted for storage. We were rarely short of meat.

Like most villages Kelfield sported a football team - of sorts. Games took place on Saturday afternoon, the only free time the players had, Sundays being sacrosanct on religious grounds. Distinguishing shirts were worn (red and white) and hob nailed boots by the majority of the players - on financial grounds. The goal posts were willow sticks surmounted by a cap or coat - there were no crossbars. The ball was of leather with an inner tube and was extremely heavy when wet. I never knew of anyone suffering from concussion when heading the ball, but looking back, it could surely of happened. Prior to the commencement of each game, the field, loaned by Mr Hare of Cordukes Farm, had to be cleared of mole hills, horse manure and cow dung. In 1929/30 the village carpenter, Mr Arthur Hare, made two regulation wooden posts which raised the stature of the village considerably.

I had two serious accidents between the ages of three and five. The first was in a field in the centre of the village, (opposite the Grey Horse), where three of my brothers were chasing a shire horse around the field. I had poked my head through a gap in the fence to see what was going on when the horse coming passed the gap kicked me on the head. I was bleeding profusely and was unconscious. My brothers, knowing they would be in trouble with my father, panicked and put me behind a wall on the opposite side of the road, next door to where my brother Sidney later lived. Fortunately, the owner of the house, Mr Pab Binns, found me in time and carried me home. The second accident happened whilst I was playing 'rounders' in the village street. The iron guttering downpipe on one of the homes fell away from the wall and hit me on the head, knocking me unconscious. In both accidents the doctor was not requested. The nearest doctor was in

Escrick, some five to six miles away and there was no telephone in the village. The doctor used a horse and trap on his visits and he was responsible for the medical requirements of several villages. It was often a long wait before he could attend you and his bills for attendance were considered to be quite high.

My father died on the 4th May 1922 from double pneumonia, at the age of forty-one years. My brother Thomas (a twin) died two weeks later on the 19th May from a motor accident, at the age of nine years. My mother having to cope with this double tragedy was in addition left with the problem of having five children under the age of fourteen who were still at school. In those days help from the State was practically nil. Help from the parish was very rarely requested as this was considered degrading and was thought to be only one step from removal to the workhouse - the nadir of one's self respect. It had not been easy for my parents to bring up a large family on one wage earner's income, but when this ceased, it was extremely difficult for my mother to manage and keep the family together. It was not unusual at this time for families in similar circumstances to ours, to disappear into the workhouse. My elder brothers, on reaching the age of eleven, helped out by working on farms after school hours and also on Saturdays. When I was just over the age of eleven, I worked on a farm (William

Dresser's) from 3.30 to 5.30 pm and then in the village grocery store from 6.00 to 8.00 pm. On Saturday's, there being no school, I worked on the farm from 7.00 to 12.00 o'clock and in the village store from 2.00 to 8.00 pm. I was paid 2s 6d (plus 1d for every twenty eggs I collected) per week by the farmer and 2s 6d (plus a quarter of sweets) per week by the store owner. Every penny we could earn was welcome and was carefully expended. From the age of five when my father died, and up to the age of thirteen, I never realised or appreciated how my mother must have suffered, how much she must have worried or how hard she had to work to make ends meet and keep the family together. I know she dreaded the thought of the family having to move into the workhouse. She must have been very close to giving up the struggle on many occasions. One occasion vividly sticks in my mind. When I was about eleven and my brother Sidney thirteen we went skating on the village pond wearing new boots which my mother had recently purchased. The ice broke and we went home with wet stockings and boots. My mother was extremely angry, normally she was very quiet and softly spoken, but on this occasion she was almost hysterical with anger. After we had taken off the wet boots, she threw one at Sidney which fortunately missed but split a small door on the sideboard. She was crying and screamed, "I wish both of you were under the sod". It was most unusual for her to lose her temper. Years later, reflecting on this incident, I realised how close she was to breaking point.

My mother had been accustomed to a hard life from childhood, having been 'hired-out' as a farm servant (commonly known as a skivvy) at the age of twelve. Her first hiring was at Mr Corduke's farm at Moor End, Kelfield - he was a distant relative. A skivvy had to do practically every type of work on the farm, both inside and outside. I remember her telling me one day that when she first started to work on this farm she had to stand on a stool to reach the table to knead the dough when baking bread. She said that she baked about fifteen large loaves at each baking session, generally every five days, for the farmer's family and for the 'living-in' labourers. She worked from 5.30am until bed time, the only free time permitted was Sunday afternoons. She continued to work as a farm servant at various farms, until she married my father in Acaster Malbis on 26th November 1902. Life had been hard for her, but now with no husband and five children still at school, it was destined to be even harder.

When I was seven years of age I remember my mother working in the potato fields 'scratting' potatoes on her knees, an old gunny sack tied around her knees to protect them and another over her shoulders whenever it rained. Other women in the 'gang' were similarly attired. The ploughman turned over the soil exposing about half of the potatoes and the women would 'scrat' in the loosened soil to pick them out. They were then placed in a basket which they pulled alongside them whilst still on their knees. When baskets were full, they were emptied by a man into a horse driven cart which followed the 'scratters'. She also worked in the turnip fields when there was frost on the ground. This was hard back-breaking work, pulling the turnip out of the hard ground, cutting off the root and the green top and placing them in line for later collection. The rate of pay for women, for potato and turnip work, was one shilling a day. In addition to the work she did outdoors, she had to feed five hungry boys. She baked at least twelve loaves of bread each week, plus pastry and cakes. The bread ration at breakfast and tea was two and a half slices per person, with margarine, dripping or home-made jam. Sunday, however, was very special. Roast beef and Yorkshire puddings for the midday meal and jelly with custard, cakes, apple or rhubarb pie, buns and farm butter instead of margarine. We were permitted one item from each plate. The normal daily basic diet consisted of bread, potatoes, rabbit and salted bacon, ham and pork from home-fed killed pigs. We also had, of course, vegetables from the garden throughout the year.

Wash day was an extremely hard day for my mother. A fire had to be lit under a copper tub in the wash-house, some distance from the house. Water had to be carried in buckets from the yard pump, or from the house water butt. After the many shirts, sheets, etc had been boiled, they were lifted out and placed in a 'peggy-tub' and manually twisted and turned by use of a three pronged wooden 'peggy' stick. After being rinsed several times with more buckets of water they were squeezed through manual operated wooden rollers and finally hung out to dry on a clothes line at the bottom of the garden, about one hundred yards from the house. Ironing by solid flat irons, heated in front of the open fire, would be done the following day, provided the clothes were sufficiently dry.

My mother attended a church service in the village school every Sunday afternoon, the parson coming from Stillingfleet since Kelfield was part of that parish. There was no music of any kind and I and my brothers, whilst under the age of fourteen, also had to attend. In the evening, winter and summer, she would walk the two miles to Stillingfleet, to attend the Methodist Chapel service and to visit her mother who lived in Stillingfleet. She always took two not over pleased sons to this service after her doctor had advised her that because of her poor health, and the possibility of her collapsing because she was very, very anaemic, she should always have someone with her.

I went to the village school, which is still standing but is now a garage, at the age of four and remained there until I was fourteen years of age. It had a total of about forty pupils aged between four and fourteen years. There were two rooms only, one for the infants and one for the older children which meant that, everyone was automatically in the top class at the age of fourteen. The school was run by two elderly ladies with the help of a trainee sixteen year old girl who helped with the infants. Both teachers lived in the adjoining school-house. Miss Dibb, the senior of the two, was of small stature, about five feet tall, slightly stooped, straight grey bobbed hair, hooked nose, wore round wire- rimmed spectacles and had a mouthful of black stumpy teeth which she appeared to be continually chewing. Miss Scott was a well built buxom woman with a pleasant personality who took a keen interest in any pupil who showed promise in their education. My brother James was given many additional hours of tuition after school hours by her. James was one of the very few pupils to ever obtain a scholarship at the village school. Unfortunately, it was beyond my mother's means to send him to a higher educational establishment. Both of these matrons were quite capable of applying the cane, Miss Scott having much the heavier hand; it was applied to the open palm of the hand.

As our cottage was a 'tied cottage' and was conditional on my father working on the owner's farm therefore, on his death it was necessary for my mother to vacate the cottage. My mother, elder brother Charles, who worked on a daily basis on one of the local farms, my brothers Albert, Sidney, David and myself, who were still attending school, moved into our third Kelfield residence when I was about seven years of age. It was a small 'not tied' terraced cottage, one of five, at Moor End in the north of the village. It had two ground floor rooms and two bedrooms plus a very small walk-in pantry. The downstairs back room was about six feet by six feet. It contained a table with a wash basin a bucket for water, a bucket for coal and a pile of kindle wood - in which the cat often eased itself. It had one very small window and a few wall pegs for coats. The front downstairs room was about eleven feet by eleven feet and was furnished with a kitchen table, a small chair, a narrow horse-hair sofa, a small sideboard, a rocking chair and a similar chair without rockers. There was a small inset cupboard in one corner for crockery and those foodstuffs which it was necessary to keep dry. On one side of the room was an open fire with an oven on the left and a hot water tank on the right. A door in one corner led to the bedrooms upstairs. The floor was of uneven red brick. A sash window provided light to the room.

The smaller of the two bedrooms was just large enough for a three and a half foot bed and a small chest of draws and had one very small window. The larger bedroom had three touching double beds, two lightweight bamboo chairs and two tin trunks for clothing. It had one large sash window. There was a chamber pot under all the beds. There was no gas, electricity or piped water - candles and paraffin lamps provided the necessary light. One outside water pump was shared by the five cottages. The toilet, our own, was a large metal bucket in an outhouse about twenty yards from the house. The out-house also contained sufficient space for bulk wood and coal, a copper tub, a 'peggy tub', a wringer with wooden rollers, a pigeon cote and a pig sty. Two pigs were generally in residence. When I was twelve years of age, being the eldest still at school, it was my job with the help of my younger brother David to empty the toilet bucket. Previously, I had carried out this duty with my elder brother Sidney, who had now left school. It had to be carried about one hundred yards along a narrow pathway, passed three houses, and finally buried in the garden. It was not a task that we enjoyed and so put it off as long as we possibly could, with the result that it was quite heavy and on occasions on the point of overflowing. We needed several rests on the way to the garden, some of which were unavoidably close to the entrances of three houses and much to the discomfort of the occupants. Being taller than my brother and because of the narrowness of the path, it was an extremely difficult load and therefore quite excusable when we dropped a few bits and pieces on the way. We finally dug a hole in the garden and emptied the contents of the bucket into it. On one occasion when we did not dig the hole sufficiently deep enough, the contents of the bucket when emptied into the hole were almost level with the surface. We camouflaged it with a thin layer of earth and trusted to fate, hoping that it would soak away. Unfortunately, my brother Charles decided to do a little gardening the following day and stepped into it, well above his ankles. I was quite surprised how lightly he took it, merely admonishing me and instructing me to ensure that I dug the hole deeper in future. I wondered if this had happened before and he considered it a natural hazard.

My mother died on 23rd July 1930. She was found unconscious and died in the early afternoon from a cerebral haemorrhage. It was my first real experience of death, for I had no recollection of my father's and brother's deaths eight years earlier. I remember cycling the two miles to Riccall to inform my uncle William, that my mother was dying in the early morning during a miserable drizzle and aware that I was in my shirt-sleeves and in considerable shock. The doctor was called from Escrick, some four miles away, coming in a pony and trap. He certified the cause of death as cerebral haemorrhage. The ritual of death in a small village then came into motion - a sad invasion of our privacy. The village undertaker, who was also the village blacksmith and joiner, did the necessary measuring-up and quickly provided a coffin - he probably kept a few standard ones in readiness. The cost of the coffin and attendance was £6 17s 6d. The cost of the wool lining, swan-down robe and burial fees was £1 7s 6d. The cost of the horse and truly conveyance to Stillingfleet was four shillings. Neighbours washed and prepared the body; there were always a few women in the village who were willing to carry out this last rite at no charge. My mother had done this on many, many occasions in the past. She was placed in the coffin and put on the bed in the large bedroom. Normally, the coffin would be placed in the Parlour, a room that was rarely used, except on special occasions such as weddings, funerals, Easter and Christmas. We had no Parlour, hence the bedroom. My younger brother David and I slept on the sofa downstairs for the next two nights. My elder brother Charles, his wife and baby, slept in the small back bedroom. My brothers Albert and Sidney, who were hired out, went back to their respective farms late at night. My brother James was serving as a soldier in India and my brother Harry was working on a farm in Canada. For the next two nights the house was unnaturally quiet, David and I spoke in whispers and moved about stunned and shocked. A considerable number of villagers came to the house to pay their last respects to my mother. She was very well known in the village and had acted as 'midwife' on many occasions, plus the laying -out procedure during her life in the village. I remember such remarks as, "She looked so lovely", and "She looked so peaceful". Prior to the lid of the coffin being screwed down, I was asked if I wanted to say goodbye. She looked years younger and as if she was just asleep. The funeral took place on the 25th July in the Parish Church at Stillingfleet. The family, close friends and many villagers, walked behind the wagon for the two miles to Stillingfleet. My Grandmother, who was eighty-one years old and quite ill, watched from her bedroom window as the cortege wended its way down the hill to the church. It was a long, long two miles. I could not take my eyes off the coffin; was she really dead? Could she still be alive? The Church service was a complete blank to me, I heard nothing the vicar or anyone else said. After the service was over, we moved over the road to the churchyard where people were gathering around the prepared grave. As the coffin was being lowered into its final resting place, I needed someone to assure me that she was really dead. My uncle William, who had always been close to my mother, gave me that assurance. After the short service at the graveside David and I slowly made our way back to Kelfield on the pathways through the fields, deep in thought and more than a little worried about the future. David and I were now orphans and still attending school. It was arranged that I should stay with my brother Charles and his wife Alice, in the same house that my mother had died in. David went to Wistow, a village four miles from Kelfield and stayed with my brother William and his wife Doris. With my mother dead, I felt that the house was no longer my home, I felt unwanted and an outsider. Years later I realised that it was not easy for my brother Charles and his wife Alice, recently married, having to put up with a thirteen year old boy. I longingly looked forward to the day when I could leave school and join the army. I had eight long months to wait. I left the village school at the Easter break following my fourteenth birthday.

Family photograph. FLP front with cat

Six youngest Price brothers, Sid, James, Albert, Thomas, Fred, David

Post card 1900/2 from FLP's Uncle William from Fatapur Sikri, India., to his sister Hannah

Post card from FLP's Aunt Zillah to her sister Hannah..."My dear Han, another boy came last Friday shall soon have plenty for a game team. What do you say." Refers to FLP birth on Friday 23rd February 1917

ENLISTMENT AGED 14 YEARS, 1931

Mr Lister, a village Market Gardener, gave me a lift on his horse-drawn wagon, he being on his way to York market to sell his weekly vegetables. He dropped me off at the entrance to the barracks in Fulford. My first impression was that the entrance looked very grim and more like an entrance to a prison than to a barracks. I signed without the slightest hesitation or concern, the Attestation paper committing myself to four years Boy Service, nine years Man Service and three years of Reserve service. A total of sixteen years of service in the King's Own Yorkshire Light Infantry, the same Regiment that my brother James had joined three years earlier and was now serving on the North West Frontier of India, in Peshawar. I was the first and only one of the family not to go immediately to farm work on leaving school.

I was given a Rail ticket for Tidworth in Wiltshire, nineteen pence ration money and one shilling for a day's pay. I left York for Tidworth about 10.00am and had to change trains four times. Prior to this journey, I had only visited York twice, Selby perhaps three or four times, even the adjacent villages of Ricall and Cawood were little known to me. Most of my life had been spent within the Parish boundary of Stillingfleet and Kelfield. I had only a very vague idea of the location of Tidworth, or its distance from York, and I had not had the time or opportunity to check prior to departing from York. I felt a little low and occasionally close to tears before reaching my destination about 7.00 o'clock in the evening. I made enquiries in a very broad Yorkshire accent, which almost needed an interpreter, as to where the KOYLI Barracks were located. They were a little over a mile from the station. It was a pleasant walk, after sitting in a train for about nine hours, and I had no luggage to carry. My worldly possessions, a pair of hob-nail boots, stockings, shorts, vest shirt, peaked cap and a jacket. I found the barracks without difficulty and reported myself to the Guardroom. A soldier of the guard escorted me to the Boy's Barrack Rooms.

Tidworth - May 1931 to 3rd March 1932

The Boy's barrack rooms were situated on the first floor of a brick built two storey block, together with a large Band practice room. The men from the Band and Bugle platoons occupied the ground floor; boys were strictly segregated from the men. The boys occupied two rooms with about twelve boys in each room, plus an NCO (Non Commissioned Officer) in each room. The barrack block was on the edge of the barrack area, conveniently adjacent to a football ground, a covered market, the garrison theatre and a quick access to Salisbury Plain. The ages of the boys were between fourteen and eighteen years, eighteen being the age when a boy came on to Man Service.

Only two other boys came from Yorkshire, Hudson from Goole and Martin from Sheffield. The remainder of the boys came from the south of England, unusual perhaps in a Yorkshire regiment, but this may have been the result of the Battalion being stationed in Dover and Blackdown prior to its move to Tidworth. I was the youngest and smallest of all the boys. A boy by the name of Farrow, who came from Croydon and was about a year older than I, took me to the company stores where I was issued with two stiffly starched sheets - with holes, three blankets, one of which was graded US and quite threadbare, for use under the mattress, a coir pillow with case, three small coir mattresses, a pair of canvas slacks and jacket and a pot mug. The remainder of my kit, I was told, would be issued the following morning. Farrow helped me to carry it, no small distance, to the barrack room and helped me to bed-down. I slept like a log on my very first night away from home.

Reveille was sounded by a bugler at 06.00am. Borrowing Farrow's towel and soap, I went into the washroom where there were about a dozen taps on a brick draining platform, and had my first wash using a tap and having an unlimited amount of clean fresh water. At home, water was drawn into a basin from a communal pump about fifty yards from the house. It was used by all members of the family and became considerably discoloured before someone volunteered to replenish it. For some trivial reason I got into an argument with the boy from Goole and had my first fight in the army. I think I was getting the worst of it before we were separated - Farrow consoled me. The Boy's paraded for physical training at 07.00am but as I had no suitable kit, I was excused.

Farrow helped me enormously to adjust to my new life, new surroundings and the language barrier; at this time I spoke with a very broad Yorkshire accent which the majority of the boys could barely understand. Farrow and I remained close friends until I was posted to India ten months later. I never met or heard of him again. In later years I always thought of him as having a similar character to the 'Artful Dodger' in 'Oliver Twist'. He had a quick and ever ready answer to every problem. I look back on our short friendship with much pleasure and considerable nostalgia.

Breakfast was at 07.45am in the HQ Company dining room, the boys having separate tables from the men. One of the mess orderlies loaned me the necessary utensils. I well remember my first breakfast in the army which consisted of two slices of bread with margarine, a plate of porridge, two bully-beef rissoles and a mug of tea. This was my first ever cooked meat breakfast. I thoroughly enjoyed it and wasted nothing for I was quite hungry having had little to eat since leaving York.

I reported to the Quartermaster's stores at 09.00am and was issued with the following...

i. A second suit of canvas overalls.
ii. 2 pairs of boots with laces.
iii. 3 pairs of grey socks.
iv. 1 forage cap with badge.
v. 1 stiff khaki cap with badge.
vi. 2 suits of khaki (which I had to take to the Regimental tailor for alteration - I was only 4ft 11ins).
vii. 1 khaki greatcoat.
viii. 2 towels (with KOYLI woven in the centre).
ix. 2 shirts.
x. 2 vests for PT.
xi. 2 vests cellular.
xii. 2 pairs blue shorts for PT.
xiii. 2 pairs cellular shorts.
xiv. 2 pairs of puttees.
xv. 1 Holdall, containing knife, fork, spoon, razor, comb, shaving brush, button brush with button stick and a tooth brush.
xvi. 1 tin of Ajax - for removing stains from uniforms.
xvii. 1 pair of very strong braces.
xviii. 1 woollen cardigan (similar to the one used by Steptoe on TV).
xix. 1 Gas mask.
xx. 1 Tin hat

xxi. 1 complete set of web equipment with water bottle.
xxii. 1 kit bag.
xxiii. 1 sea kit bag.
xxiv. 1 pair of gloves.
xxv. 1 balaclava.
xxvi. 1 brass bed docket.
xxvii. 1 regimental cane.
xxviii. 1 white buff belt

To reduce the chances of theft, every item had to be stamped with my regimental number (4688132) prior to leaving the store. This numbering, plus measurement for the extensive alterations required to this mountain of kit, required a barrack box which fitted under the bed, a kit bag, a small locker on the wall behind my bed, two wall pegs for the web equipment and a wall shelf for my greatcoat, mess tin, spare puttees and tin hat. I made a quick trip to the covered market before dinner and purchased metal polish, boot polish, toothpaste, white and green blanco and a comic, the 'Bullseye'- the first comic I had ever purchased.

The barrack room was sparsely furnished but extremely clean. In the centre of the room was a six foot trestle table with two six foot forms, scrubbed white, a large black cast iron coal bin, a broom, two handed scrubbing brushes and one long handled heavily weighted dry scrubber. The room had one fireplace and the beds were of iron with slats. When not in use as beds they were reduced to half their size by sliding the front half of the bed under the rear half. For morning inspection they were reduced, blankets and sheets folded at the head of the bed surmounted by a towel, a white blanco belt and a personalised brass name plate showing name, initials, number and religion. Everyone in the room was allocated a room job by the NCO (None Commissioned Officer eg. Corporal or Sergeant) the youngest boys got the worst jobs. Mine, I was immediately informed, was to clean two large sash windows by using metal polish which I had to provide. It was a tedious job and gave me a lifelong dislike to cleaning windows. Every Friday evening the room was hand scrubbed and to ensure that it was immaculately clean for the Saturday morning inspection, each boy provided a blanket to cover the freshly scrubbed floor until reveille the following morning. I often missed the loss of this blanket during the winter.

Dinner, at 12.45pm, was a large plate of stew, a slice of bread, rice pudding and a mug of tea. I thoroughly enjoyed it and wasted nothing. At 13.45pm, I was on my first parade with nineteen other KOYLI boy soldiers and marched to the Garrison Education Centre for tuition in 3rd, 2nd and 1st certificates of education; I was going for the 3rd, the lowest. As the order of dress was 'clean fatigue' (canvass), I was in uniform for the first time; it was also the first time I had worn long pants. About fifty or sixty other boy soldiers, from other units in Tidworth, were already at the centre when we arrived. I was getting a little nervous and perturbed. The instructor of my class was a Corporal and the first lesson was on map reading. I had never seen an Ordinance Survey map, or more correctly, any map. I had no idea what a protractor was or what it was used for. I had never heard of spot heights, contours, viaducts or any of the other legends for reading a map. The whole subject was a mystery to me. I was, to put it mildly, utterly confused, miserable and feeling considerably inferior. It was just three days since I had left the small village school in Kelfield, a place that now seemed a thousand miles away and in a different world to that in which I now found myself. I had a lot to learn. The lesson, about an hour and a half, passed without any great embarrassment - much to my relief. Youth, however, is very resilient and I quickly recovered from my depression and inferiority complex. After a few more trips to the Education Centre I began to find it quite interesting and not in the least boring; I was learning something new. Some four months later I passed the necessary examination which was very basic. I felt very elated at my success and seeing my name published in Battalion Orders, it added at least one inch to my chest measurement. Several of the other boys failed the examination which made me feel quite superior. Tea was at 16.00pm and consisted of two slices of bread with margarine and jam and a mug of tea. I heard many of the soldiers grumbling about the food. For myself, I had no complaints whatever was on the menu and I enjoyed it. I was always hungry and if there were any 'spares' going, I was quickly into the queue.

With the help of my friend Farrow, I quickly got into the day-to-day routine. Reveille at 6.00am was followed by muster parade at 07.00 am for drill, sport, fatigues or generally weeding the Company area. Breakfast at 07.45am, music instruction from 09.00am to 12.00 noon, dinner at 12.45pm, physical training at the Garrison Gymnasium twice a week 14.00 to 15.00pm, religious instruction in the church rooms once a week 14.00 to 15.00pm, plus Sunday morning Church Parade and Sunday evening Church Service. The authorities, apparently, considered that we needed lots of religious instruction. Any spare time in the afternoons was given to musical instruction. Tea was at 16.00pm when generally the day's duties ended. I quickly adjusted to my new lifestyle and with the help of Farrow I learnt how to clean my web equipment, spit and polish (horn) my boots, make up my bed, lay out my kit for inspection, put on my puttees (a complicated procedure because of my small thin legs), press my trousers by wetting the insides of the creases with soap and then placing them folded under my bed sheets at night and drying them with the heat of my body. He also warned me to be extra careful of Bandsmen who would be after my ring (anus). One he especially named was Cutler, who was a veteran 1914-18 soldier with horrible hooded and lecherous eyes.

I sold my civilian jacket and shorts to 'Ma', an elderly woman running the Regimental canteen, for sixty slices of fried bread, two per day for a month for Farrow and myself. We also cut the grass in the Roman Catholic churchyard for a fried egg sandwich. We would have liked the grass to grow much quicker than it did, for more egg sandwiches. Because of my small and skinny body, I was instructed by the Sergeant Major of Head Quarter's Company, a burley six foot plus man by the name of Grant, to report to the Sergeants Mess daily at 20.00pm when the cook would give me a supper from whatever had been left over from the Sergeants dinner. This continued for about five months, when I suppose the Sergeant Major considered that I had started to grow and to put on some weight.

I had to attend the Garrison Dental Centre every day for a week because I required lots of treatment, fillings and extractions. I had very rarely ever used a toothbrush, with the result that my teeth were in a very poor condition. After all these years, I still vividly remember that there were three dental chairs close together in a very busy dental centre. When a chair became vacant, the new occupant, as he walked in, got a clear and unpleasant view of two squirming patients. I had a very painful and miserable week and was very pleased when it was all over. Following this experience I started to clean my teeth every morning.

Tidworth was basically an Army training camp, situated in the open country of Salisbury Plain and ideal for military training. There were practically no civilians based in the barrack area since nearly all work, (cooking, cleaning, hair cutting and all fatigues), were carried out by soldiers. Adjacent to the KOYLI barracks were the Scots Grays, a famous heavy cavalry regiment. A little further on a regiment of Hussars, a regiment of Lancers and another regiment of infantry, the KRRC (Kings Royal Rifle Corps). At any one time there must have been at least 1000 to 2000 horses exercising in and around Tidworth plus two infantry units, each about 800 strong. Everywhere you went, you saw khaki.

There were two cinemas in Tidworth, a military one in the barracks and a civilian one in the village - both were talkies. The one in the barracks was not very comfortable, the seating consisting of wooden forms and light wire chairs. The one in the village, run by civilians, had fixed plush comfortable chairs and was much cleaner and better organised - 95% of the occupants were however, soldiers in uniform. The cost of a ticket for a boy was 3 pence. I had never been to a 'Talkie', and only once to a silent movie, in my life and was thrilled and excited at the prospect of seeing generally two films every week. I could easily afford it as I was careful with my pay of three shillings per week, the balance of four shillings (my pay being seven shillings) was held in credit for when I would be going on furlough, or charged with stoppages for replacement of kit. I also opened a Post Office savings account into which I paid 6 pence a week. I learned to read music and to play the clarinet to some small degree. After learning the necessary scales, I was able to play the average straight forward tunes, "Lady of Spain" being my favourite and one of the easiest. I enjoyed the Battalion route marches, football with real (borrowed) football boots, going to inter-unit boxing competitions and to the various venues as a fatigue man where the Band had engagements. A real treat, was the annual Army Tattoo held in Tidworth, which was very realistic and on a grand spectacular scale. Life was beginning to be good and interesting. I had money in my pocket for the first time in my life and I had plenty to eat.

I was granted eight days Christmas furlough from Tidworth in December 1931. My brother Sidney, who had joined the KOYLI on 22nd June 1931, was granted furlough from Pontefract, the KOYLI depot, but my brother

Albert who had joined the KOYLI on 11th December 1931 was not allowed furlough as he had not completed sufficient basic training. Sidney and I billeted ourselves on my brother Charles in Kelfield. As most of our former friends were working, we spent most of the working day in the 'Grey Horse' playing cards and dominoes. Although I was not yet fifteen years of age, I was in the King's uniform and fully accepted as being entitled to enter the 'Grey horse' and drink whatever I fancied. I took no interest in girls. I had developed, during my eight months in the south, something of a cockney accent which amused my former friends. I no longer said 'watter' but water, 'briard' but bread, 'booit' but boot and 'stoan' but stone, to mention but a few of the changes I had unconsciously adopted.

We had an excellent Christmas with my brother Charles and his wife Alice. She was a very good cook having worked on a farm as a 'skivvy' from the age of fourteen years. We had home fed goose, which I killed, and home-made Christmas pudding with custard. Sidney and I provided the drinks. The evening was spent in the 'Grey Horse'. On Boxing Day, Charles, Sidney and I cycled to Wistow and spent the day and the night with my brother William, his wife Doris and my younger brother David, who was still attending school in Wistow. Sidney had a little too much to drink and on endeavouring, though very unsteadily, to light the candles on the Xmas tree, managed to set the curtains alight. Fortunately, not much damage was done. Late in the evening, Doris's brother arrived from their farm on Bishop Dyke to say that their mother had just died. Although her early death had been expected it still, understandably, put a considerable gloom on the party. We played cards until the early morning, having mad periodic trips to the back door of the 'Black Swan' for additional supplies of beer. On arrival back in Kelfield at about 08.00am, Charles was met by a very annoyed Alice who was understandably very upset at not knowing the reason for his all night absence. As there was no telephone in the village it had not been possible for Charles to let her know that he was spending the night in Wistow, which was his excuse - albeit a poor one. At breakfast, she threw a tin of milk at him, which caught him on the head and drew blood. Sidney didn't help the situation by saying," she is only playing", and that he should have ducked. Sidney and I were amused at the situation for a while, but eventually got bored and went for a cycle ride to the "Cocked Hat" plantation to see if we could catch a rabbit or a pheasant. The eight days slowly dragged by, but I was restless and bored and was not sorry when my furlough ended - it was a much more interesting life in Tidworth.

I had only been back in Tidworth for two or three weeks when I was informed that sometime in the near future I was to be posted to the 2nd Battalion KOYLI in India. Quite a shock! I would be given fourteen days leave prior to my departure. A week or two later I was ordered to report to the Military Hospital for a TAB injection, dental and other medical checks. (A TAB injection is given to provide immunity against - typhoid, paratyphoid A and paratyphoid B) The TAB injection gave me a very stiff arm and considerable pain for a day or two. A few days later, I was given fourteen days Leave, fourteen days pay at 1s per day and fourteen days ration money at 10 1/2 pence per day and a return rail ticket for York. Charles and Alice were very surprised to see me back so soon. My fourteen days passed slowly and without event, everyone I knew appeared to be at work or in school. I reported to the Military Hospital in York, as I had been instructed to do, on the eighth day after my first TAB, for a second TAB, it being necessary for me to have the two TAB's prior to embarkation. The vicar, Reverend Chapple, invited me to the vicarage to have tea with him, his wife and sixteen year old daughter. It was a very pleasant and enjoyable surprise. I had known him all my life and I had been in his choir since I was eleven years old. He had travelled in the Far East and had spent several years in Japan. He was very interested in my forthcoming posting to India and warned me of the hazards and dangers I would eventually encounter. I was not aware of the dangers he was referring to - but a few years later I got a rough idea. I regret that I never had the pleasure of meeting him again. I visited my brother David in Wistow where he had settled down quite happily, and thanked my brother Charles and sister-in-law Alice for my stay in Kelfield and was on my way back to Tidworth and the future.

The day after I arrived in Tidworth, I was informed that I was to sail on the HMT Nevasa, leaving Southampton on the 4th March, which gave me about four days before departure. I collected my tropical KD uniform (Khaki drill) and various other items of clothing from the Quartermaster's stores, which added to the mountain of kit which I already possessed. I closed my small Post Office account - with the thought that I would treat Farrow and myself to an egg sandwich for supper, for the next three nights. My difficulty was going to be packing all my kit into one main kit-bag, one small kit-bag, my web pack and my haversack. My main kit-bag would be stored in the main baggage hold on the ship and I would not see it again until arriving in Bombay, in a little over three weeks. Everything I needed on board had to be packed in the small sea kit-bag and my pack and haversack.

A large draft of soldiers from the Kings Royal Rifle Corps was to leave Tidworth on the same troop train that I was booked on. The very tall (6ft 2in) Company Sergeant Major (CSM) Grant walked with me to the rail station. He carried my main kit-bag (most unusual), and I carried the small sea kit-bag and was wearing full web equipment with pack, haversack and rolled greatcoat on the top of the pack. We must have looked quite odd, a 6ft-2in soldier and a 5ft Boy soldier - my pack must have been below my backside. The CSM saw me safely seated on the train and wished me a safe journey. He was a very popular and well liked CSM, about to complete his 22 years in the Army. On arrival at Southampton I staggered off the train onto the platform where my identity was checked and confirmed. I followed the file of soldiers boarding the ship, staggered up the gangway then down some steps to a lower deck where I stacked my kit and awaited orders.

I did not see the Nevasa raise anchor and leave the dock area for I was below deck looking for somewhere to sleep and somewhere to eat. I asked several NCO's among the crowded soldiers if they knew where I could go for information regarding my allocated billet, but I was totally unsuccessful. I made myself comfortable in a corner near my kit and waited for someone to find me. I was the only soldier (OR -Other Ranks) from the KOYLI on board except for a Major Walker and his wife and a Sergeant Clarke and his wife. Sergeant Clarke's wife contracted measles soon after coming on board and both were placed under quarantine for the rest of the voyage. On reaching the open channel we ran into a violent storm and I was very, very seasick. There were about a thousand soldiers on board plus a few officers and their families. I don't know how well those in cabins fared, but those on the troop decks suffered 100% severe seasickness. Latrines and wash areas were permanently crowded to capacity with vomiting sick soldiers. The decks were covered in vomit and the smell was awful. The conversation was limited to, 'Roll on bloody Bombay'. The storm lasted for about three days and nights. On reaching calmer waters near Gibraltar I began to feel much better and for a second time started to look for a Mess table and something to eat. I felt very hungry, having eaten practically nothing for three days. I tried two or three Mess tables unsuccessfully before begrudgingly being accepted as a temporary member – 'for the time being'. Besides surprising them on the amount of food this 'little bugger', as I was called, could put away – my appearance could not have impressed them for I had not washed for three days. I thoroughly enjoyed my meal, porridge – as much as I could eat, bread, kippers and tea. On entering the Mediterranean big improvements took place with discipline and administration becoming the order of the day. The troops found their sea-legs and came back to life. Boat drill, life-jacket drill and Ship inspection were held every morning by the ship's Captain and the senior Military Officer, with a long tail of junior military officials. As I had no idea as to where I should attend, I just attached myself to the nearest squad available when I heard the bugle sounding Stations. It was another two days before someone from Administration found me and allocated me a permanent Boat Drill Station and my correct Mess table with soldiers of the KRRC. Various duties for Guards, Fatigues, Orderlies, etc were nominated for the day, a week or for the duration of the voyage. I was detailed to act as Batman to Major Walker (KOYLI) - the major must have arranged this himself so that he could keep an eye on me. The only work I did, if it could be called work, was to polish his buttons on his uniform and Greatcoat. But, I was now a Batman and I felt at least two inches taller. The most disliked fatigue was that of potato peeling, of which tons of them were required daily. Twenty men were detailed for it and it lasted all morning, or until the required amount was peeled. The most difficult duty was that of Mess Orderly - two required from each table. They had to collect the containers of food from the Galley, issue it out, clean up the table area and return the cleaned containers to the Galley. Difficult enough on a steady rolling ship but during rough seas, almost impossible. There were many occasions when the containers came tumbling down the steep steps, followed by the Orderly. If there were no volunteers to do the duty, then everyone would have to take their turn.

Fortunately, two hard-up men volunteered, after everyone on the table had agreed to pay them one day's pay. They were also excused all other duties and fatigues during the rest of the voyage. My contribution was one shilling.

The daily routine was Reveille at 06.00am. Hammocks with two blankets had to be neatly rolled and deposited into the bowels of the ship for storage before breakfast. There was always a long queue and the lower one went, the more stuffy and smelly was the air; and the more the ship appeared to roll. If the hammock was not rolled satisfactorily you were sent back upstairs to rectify. I only did this double journey once, and you never got the same hammock again. At the age of 15, I never gave a thought to ring-worms, crabs, wet-dreams or ex VD sufferers. Washing facilities were quite inadequate. Many of the soldiers got up hours before Reveille, to wash and shave before the majority started. I was lazy, did not need to shave and didn't bother too much if I had to put up with a quick lick of a wash. Breakfast was at 07.45am and consisted of porridge, various kinds of fish, sausage or bacon and eggs, tea, freshly baked bread and margarine. The mid-day meal consisted of various named stews, all tasting the same, rice pudding, stewed prunes or 'spotted dick' as afters. Tea consisted of bread, margarine, jam, and on occasions, fish. Once I had recovered from my sea-sickness, I possessed an insatiable appetite. I ate everything with relish that was on offer.

Boat Drill and Life Jacket Drill took place every morning. When this was completed, there were fatigues such as potato peeling, galley duties, cleaning the wash rooms and toilets of the Officers and families, carrying items of food from storage in the bowels of the ship to the Galley, biscuits, cigarettes and chocolate to the Canteen. The peeling of the potatoes was the most disliked of all the fatigues as it seemed to be never ending. Sufficient potatoes had to be peeled for over 1,500 people. Some days we had baked potatoes, in their skins, for dinner and no-one ever complained for this fatigue. All open decks and the Troop Heads were washed down daily with sea water by the ship's crew, plus also sanding them twice a week. Physical training took place every morning before breakfast and normally lasted for about thirty minutes. The air felt so fresh and so clean, especially after spending the night in a very crowded and smelly Mess deck. I felt good and was looking forward to breakfast.

There was only one film on board, 'The Speckled Band'. It was shown on the promenade deck, two or three times a week. By the time we reached Bombay (three weeks), I think everyone had seen it. Boxing competitions, which were very popular, were held between the thirty or more Units represented on board. They took place on the forward ship's deck twice a week. The deck was filled to its utmost on these occasions, plus all vantage places overlooking the deck, were quickly filled. There were two 'Grudge fights' on this voyage, between those who had been caught fighting/ brawling and had agreed to settle their differences in the ring with boxing gloves over three rounds each of three minutes. The spectators liked it, the umpire and the three judges controlled it quite well, and the contestants appeared to be satisfied.

The Nevasa was coal fired, old and slow. In good weather she managed to travel a little over 300 miles a day, but in rough weather it was down to 180 miles. She took three days to reach Gibraltar, another six to reach Port Said where we berthed to take on fuel, water and supplies. The coal came on board in small baskets carried by menial workers, on their heads, each basket containing about forty pounds of coal. Loading went on all day for three days. The carriers came up one gang-plank, emptied their baskets into the coal bunker and left by another gang-plank. It was a continuous stream and went on from early morning to late at night. At the end of the three days, the ship was black with coal dust. Vendors in small boats selling silks, fruits, carvings, books, dirty postcards and aphrodisiacs of doubtful quality, surrounded the ship for three days. Bartering between the vendors and the troops was vigorous and rude with cheating taking place on both sides. It was sometimes necessary for the ship's Regimental police to intervene when arguments became too heated, the police normally settling the argument by emptying buckets of water over the offending vendor until he retired. They appeared to accept this treatment as one of the hazards of their trade and were back haggling for more trade within a matter of minutes. All the vendors understood and spoke sufficient English to carry out their trade. Small Egyptian boys, about six or seven years of age, encouraged the troops to throw coins into the water, for which they would dive and show off their skill by retrieving them. For the promise of a few coins, some of these youngsters swam under the Nevasa, emerging at the other side, quite a feat.

A most welcome break from the restricted life on board was a route march of about five miles in and around Port Said. It was a wonderful feeling to stretch one's legs and feel one's feet on firm ground again. I found the strange flat top buildings, open road-side shops, the smells, the dress of the inhabitants, the horse drawn vehicles, the terribly over-laden bow-legged donkeys and the chatter of a foreign language, quite fascinating. Vendors of dirty postcards and doubtful powders and liquids to improve one's manhood pestered the marchers throughout the march.

Every day brought a new experience. I had never been on a sea going ship in my life,

I had never seen a black coloured person in my life and I had never set foot in a foreign country before. Life was good and exciting – I could cope. I had money in my pocket and the food was good and plentiful. I have been to Port Said several times since but all subsequent visits did not have the magic of this my first visit. We changed into tropical uniform (Khaki Drill) on leaving Port Said.

We spent three very pleasant and leisurely days in the Suez Canal, and it's three lakes, Mansala, Timsah and Bitter, which I found to be much larger than I expected. We spent many hours at anchor in these lakes, waiting for ships travelling north to emerge from the canal before we could enter and proceed south. The actual canal was quite narrow, which meant that our speed, to avoid damage to the banks, was extremely slow. A road ran alongside the whole of the canal, which gave us a small but interesting view of Egyptian life and its travelling inhabitants. A magnificent statue of the builder, Ferdinand De Lessops, was of considerable interest to most of the soldiers as every 2nd and 3rd Army Certificate of Education contained questions of this man and the building of the canal. The canal reduced the journey to India from six weeks to three weeks.

After leaving the Suez Canal, our next port of call was Port Sudan, about half way, 700 miles, down the Red Sea, for the disembarkation of troops for duty in the Sudan. We dropped anchor for about three hours, just long enough for those who wished to take the opportunity for a quick dip in the sea. The water was warm, clean and extremely clear. PT shorts, as issued by the army, were worn as swim suits. I thoroughly enjoyed splashing about even though I could not swim at this time. I particularly remember the very large amounts of coral which were of many varied and marvellous colours. The Port Sudan natives (who were nick-named Fuzzy Wuzzies) intrigued me considerably for I had learned from my army history that they had broken a fully active service British Square at a battle in the Sudan in the 19thCentury. The ones I saw were of medium height, I had expected them to be taller, well built and with an enormous mass of solid black curly hair, which they lazily and continually prodded with a piece of pointed wood. Their heads with the matted hair were much wider than their shoulders. We took a little over four days to steam through the Red Sea and except for the heat and the fatigues, it was quite enjoyable. Massive shoals of flying fish, glittering in the strong sunlight, swam and flew alongside the ship for mile after mile. I never tired of watching these fish as they flew above the water; I continually picked one out from the rest as it appeared to fly further than the others. Silent and deadly looking sharks also swam alongside the ship, waiting for the remnants of meals thrown from the galley. Our next port of call was Aden where a number of troops were disembarked for service in Aden and the adjacent states. Mail was also delivered and collected but, there was no opportunity to go ashore here for we only stopped for about two hours and were soon on our way to the Arabian Sea, next stop Bombay.

We were in the Arabian Sea (Indian Ocean) for six days and saw no land during this time. The sea was extremely calm and looked more like a lake or an enormous pond rather than an ocean. The six days were rather long and dragged by rather monotonously. PT, fatigues and inspections were tolerably accepted without complaint, the monotony was broken one day when we passed within hailing distance of a troop ship on it's way home to England with 'old soldiers' who had completed their six to seven years in the Far East. Hundreds of pith hats were thrown toward our ship by the old soldiers together with some remarks regarding our future. This brief encounter did make one realise that it would be six or seven years before we would be in a similar position to those old soldiers. The day after we had passed the homeward bound troopship, a soldier jumped or fell overboard. The Nevasa made a very belated and slow turn and circled where it was thought the soldier would be, but without success.

Marine life was large, varied and in abundance. There was a continuous stream of porpoises on both sides of the ship from morning to night, lots of beautiful coloured flying fish, sharks and several schools of whales. Whilst on my embarkation leave in England I had visited Scarborough and had paid two pence to see a whale that had been caught in the North Sea off Scarborough. I was in uniform and the seaman giving the lecture on the whale, on spotting me said, " Very few of you will ever see another whale like this one, except that young lad in uniform when he goes to India". I remembered those words as I watched these giant creatures swimming within a few hundred yards of the ship. The weather was hot and humid and I spent most of my leisure time reading. Everyone who could find the necessary deck space, slept on deck, which necessitated a quick move before Reveille as the lascar crew commenced washing down the deck at 6.00am sharp.

On landing in Bombay, we quickly disembarked and were marched a few hundred yards to the railway yards where troop trains were assembled to convey the troops to the various cantonments scattered throughout the Indian sub-continent. At this time India included Pakistan, Bangladesh, Sri Lanka and Burma. This was the first occasion when I could, with certainty, confirm that the Scottish soldier did not, in hot weather, wear anything under his kilt. There were about fifty to sixty Scottish soldiers sitting on the embankment waiting to entrain as I walked passed at the bottom of the embankment. The sight was unforgettable, and I don't know why, but I thought of the days when I collected the eggs on the farm at home and saw the lines of roosters perched in the hen-houses.

MY FIRST JOURNEY IN A TROOP TRAIN

BOMBAY TO AGRA

I commenced my journey to Agra on a troop train, together with well over 500 troops from various regiments who were destined for military stations and cantonments dotted all over the whole Indian sub-continent. To the best of my memory there were nine or ten carriages making up the train. Each carriage being sixty or seventy feet long had ten or eleven compartments and one toilet and one wash-basin with a corridor connecting the compartments. Each compartment was about 4ft 6in wide and 6ft 3in in length and was the authorised travelling space for six soldiers, for eating, sleeping and their full web equipment. There was a small electric fan in each compartment and one had to be very careful when standing up otherwise you had a haircut. The compartments were not enclosed but separated by iron stanchions to allow the air, and the smells, to circulate freely throughout the whole carriage. A collapsible table was erected in the centre of the compartment for meals and when not in use it was clipped to the side of the corridor. On each side of the compartment were three slatted wooden bunks. The two higher and two lower ones were fixed and immovable, the centre ones being dropped during the day to make sitting room for the six occupants, three on each side. At night, if using the centre or lower bunk, and if being of normal stature, it was necessary to partly ease oneself out of the bunk before turning over. There were two narrow windows in each compartment each having three exchangeable types of fitting, glass, wire mesh and wooden louvers, and all lockable from the inside. These were necessary because of the wide variations of temperature, dust storms, mosquitoes etc. plus the large numbers of thieves looking for easy pickings whenever the train was halted at night and the occupants asleep. The toilet, about 2ft 6in by 2ft 6in was a hole in the floor, which proved to be not large enough if the user had a stomach upset or was in a hurry because of the queue waiting outside. After the first day, one had to be extremely careful where you placed your feet as several visitors had missed the vital spot. The wash room, if it could be called a room, was of the same size as the toilet and had a fixed basin with a tap. After one day travelling, we ran out of water, which cut out all washing and increased the smell from the toilet which began to look more like a midden.

Troop trains, unless the journey was in aid of the civil power, gave right of way to civilian trains, hence the often long and tedious journeys and the long stops in railway sidings. The temperature must have been close to 100*F in the shade and when the train stopped for any length of time the heat was almost unbearable. This journey, my first of many across India, if it had not been so uncomfortable could have been like a fairy tale come to life. Some of the rural villages we passed gave the appearance of belonging to a long gone age and reminded me of the biblical pictures from my Sunday school days.

Breakfast, eaten in very cramped conditions, consisted of a tin of corned beef, a tin of margarine and a loaf of bread for each compartment of six soldiers, plus a mug of tea per person. The corned beef was warm and mushy because of the heat, but I still enjoyed it. The tea made with condensed milk was most welcome and very refreshing. After breakfast, the five men in the compartment started playing cards for money. I had a little money, but was not inclined to risk losing it so I sat in the seat near the corridor and had a good view of the Indian landscape as the train steadily sped along. I was fascinated by the strangeness of the dress of the people, the slow moving bullock carts, the mangy looking dogs, the pathetic beggars, the extensively veiled women, and the very crowded stations.

There was one stop for a hot meal around midday, stew and a chapatti followed by rice pudding with dried fruit. The beggars that quickly surrounded the stationary train were given a large proportion of the meal by the sympathetic soldiers who had never seen such thin and starving old men and women and naked pot-bellied children. Mangy and miserable thin dogs with half of their fur missing trotted up and down looking for scraps. Later in the day, about 6.00pm, we stopped for tea which had been prepared by the staff at one of the cantonments we passed through. A loaf of bread, a tin of jam and a tin of margarine were distributed to each compartment; we queued up on the platform for a mug of tea which was very welcome and most refreshing, not withstanding the high temperature. On the second day when we stopped for the midday meal, I had collected my plate of stew and chapatti, (A chapatti is something like a thick lump of Yorkshire pudding), and was on my way back to the train when I heard a rushing noise, a momentary glimpse of a dark shadow, and my chapatti was no longer on my plate - a kite (known to the troops as a shite hawk) had taken advantage of my inexperience. Later when I arrived in Agra, one of the old soldiers told me to always keep my hand moving from side to side over my plate, which deterred the hawks.

We considered ourselves very cramped and uncomfortable in our train, but whenever we were passed by civilian trains we began to consider that we were travelling in luxury. Many of the civilian trains had more passengers on the roof and sides of the train than were packed inside. The trains gave the appearance of being an enormous human centipede. Vendors of every description plied their wares on the platforms of the stations selling nuts, milk and a large variety of fruit, betel nut, tea, cold drinks, books and papers. All was a little basic perhaps and not too hygienic, but on the whole everything that the western or eastern traveller could desire. The troops were strictly forbidden to purchase any type of food or drink - this was enforced by lots of military police. All the women, except the beggar women, were heavily veiled from head to foot, the only visible part of their body being their feet; even their eyes were not visible. The larger railway stations we passed through at night had the platforms packed tight with sleeping figures stretched out on the bare ground with but a flimsy thin cloth covering them, all presumably waiting for the next day's train.

I left the troop train on its arrival in Delhi and was given a second class ticket by Movement Control, for a civilian train going to Agra, a distance of about 130 miles. My compartment, shared with four Indians, was quite luxurious when compared to the troop train. I had four times as much room and there were good washing facilities and toilets. The toilet mystified me at first then greatly amused me. Inquisitively, pressing one of the adjacent handles whilst sitting on the seat, I was greatly surprised by a spout of water shooting up my backside - water not paper. I spent most of my time keenly observing with great interest the passing countryside, its people, transport, animals and its mud built houses. The train made several stops before reaching Agra and at one of the stops I took the opportunity to buy two oranges. There were no military police on this train and I think I was the only military person on it. I bought only the oranges, remembering the warning given to the troops on leaving Bombay with regard to contaminated fruit and its resultant dysentery. The journey to Agra took about four hours; a long four hours for I had very little conversation with my fellow travellers. There were two rail stations in Agra in 1932, the City and the Cantonment; my ticket was for the Cantonment. I was in a very dirty and scruffy condition. My drill uniform had been worn daily for about two weeks in high temperatures and in sweaty crowded conditions - it showed signs of accidents with spilled stew, jam and other items of food so it was in dire need of washing.

On the platform I was confronted by a horde of coolies all wanting to carry my bags to the transport outside the station. With considerable hesitation I selected one, ensuring he was never out of my sight until we reached the tongas (a vehicle drawn by one horse) outside the station. I think I paid him two annas (2 pence) - one sixth of a day's pay. I had no difficulty, but again misgivings in hiring transport to take me to the barracks for there were large numbers of available tongas whose vociferous drivers vied with each other for my custom. I selected one that spoke a little English. My kit, consisting of one large kitbag, a small sea kitbag, marching order and rolled great coat strapped to my pack, all of which was loaded by the driver onto the front seat next to where he was sitting. I sat on the double seat facing the rear which was clean and very comfortable. The driver, who spoke a little English, pointed out various landmarks of interest, called me Sahib and kept the pony going at a very brisk trot for the two mile journey to barracks. He charged me four annas and took me right up to the barrack block occupied by the advance party of the Battalion which was still in Peshawar. He could easily have charged me more for he could clearly see that I was a raw recruit to the Raj, but he treated me with respect and I am certain, with considerable sympathy because of my small stature and age.

It was on the last day of March when I arrived at Akbar Barracks. The unit, to which I had been posted, 2nd Battalion Kings Own Yorkshire Light Infantry, was still in Peshawar on the north-west frontier of India. They eventually arrived in Agra on 7th of April. There was, however, a small advance party of about thirty men from the Battalion in Agra when I arrived. Their job was to earmark the various barrack rooms, wash houses, cook house, offices, etc, prior to the arrival of the Battalion. On the advice of a soldier of the advance party I handed over my KD slacks and jacket, which were extremely dirty, to the local dhobi. I was very surprised when both items were returned within two hours, washed, ironed and not a stain anywhere. The charge was two annas (2 pence). I was issued with two blankets, three very good new sheets, three coir mattresses, a coir pillow and a mosquito net and told which barrack block to bed down in. It was a block with sufficient accommodation for 120 men and I was the only person to be sleeping in it for over a week. Men and boys were rigidly separated in the army. After making my bed down and hanging my mosquito net, ensuring it was tucked in under the mattresses as I had been instructed, I went to the wash room and had a thoroughly enjoyable cold shower. Dressed in my newly laundered KD, I reported to the cookhouse at about 8.00pm, for a belated tea cum supper consisting of, bread and butter, pork rissoles, rice pudding and a mug of tea. I was given as much as I could eat.

After a short explorative and inquisitive walk around the immediate vicinity, I found the tree rats (squirrels) and the bird life very interesting, after which I went to my bed block. I was extremely tired but found that sleep did not come easily since my mind was filled with the events of the last three days. At 10.15pm, when every light had been switched off, my imagination ran riot. I imagined snakes slithering across the floor, scorpions emerging from the walls and other strange eastern crawly things around my bed. I could hear the incessant buzz of mosquitoes endeavouring to pierce my net - I had been warned to ensure that no part of my body was in contact with the sides of the net, for it was quite easy for the mosquitoes to bite through the net. In the distance I could hear the local Mullah intoning his prayers; it sounded strangely weird and did not improve my uneasiness before finally falling asleep. I awoke quite early next morning feeling refreshed and a little ashamed of myself for my unease during the night. Everything looked much different in daylight and after washing I reported to the cookhouse and ate with considerable relish a large breakfast of porridge, pork rissoles, a fried egg, bread and butter and a mug of tea. Later in the day I bought an air pistol from one of the soldiers in the advance party for the sum of one rupee (1shilling and 4 pence) and spent many hours shooting at crows, buzzards, kite hawks, tree rats and parakeets. Large flocks of parakeets flew over the barrack area every evening, presumably to their roosting grounds. One day I decided to go to the Barrah (big) Bazaar, which was about two miles from the barracks, to replenish my dwindling stock of ammunition. On arrival at the outskirts of the bazaar, which looked very crowded and sounded very noisy, I became a little worried and concerned, so turned back for the barracks. There were no Europeans about, the environment was strange, everyone appeared to stare at me and I realised the language difficulty. I felt very small - much less than my five feet, and very much alone. One of the cooks obtained some ammunition for me the following day. I spent the next few days, until the arrival of the Battalion, mostly on my own except at meal times when I messed with the men. Men and boys did not fraternise.

On 7th April, or thereabouts, I watched the Battalion about eight hundred strong march into the barracks led by the Band and the Buglers and commanded by Lieutenant Colonel E.B.J. Tagg, a tall, extremely dark and thin officer of fierce military bearing. The soldier's uniforms were stained with sweat and they were very sun-tanned and very fit and healthy. I followed Head Quarters Company (HQ Company) to their allotted barrack block and watched them make a mess of the drill manoeuvre of Piling Arms. There was some excuse for this as it was a complicated movement which was very rarely carried out. My brother James (4687170) was in HQ Company employed as a printer in the Printer's Shop. He had been posted to the 2nd Battalion in 1929. He was extremely pleased to see me and bombarded me with questions regarding the family in England. Our mother had died in 1930 whilst he was in Peshawar on the North West Frontier and the family had partly broken up on her death. He was not aware that I had joined the Army and was further surprised when I told him that brothers Sidney and Albert had also joined. Letter writing was not a strong point in the Price family. We did not have time to talk for very long as he had to find his allocated bed space, draw his bedding and his kit-bag from the baggage A T Cart and place his rifle in the steel lock-up rifle rack. Security of arms was very strict.

HQ Company consisted of a Signal Platoon, Band, Buglers, Boys, employed men such as Cooks, Printers, Regimental Police, pioneers and a small Headquarters. The barrack block allocated to Headquarters Company, which was the one I had slept in, was about 400 feet long, fifty feet wide and at its highest point was about twenty-five feet high and was built to accommodate 120 men. The inner sleeping area was about twenty-one feet wide and had two long lines of punkahs extended for the full length of the block. Surrounding this inner area was an integral walled outer room, ten feet wide, which was used for dining purposes and for emergency overspill sleeping accommodation. Surrounding this outer room was a ten feet wide covered-in veranda. All walls were very thick and except for the inner wall of the veranda, which had wooden doors, consisted of high open archways about ten feet apart. At one end of the block there was a small storeroom and an office. The complete block was surrounded by five or six red sandstone steps. This type of barrack block was standard in the majority of cantonments on the plains of India. They were built in the late 19th Century and were designed with the object of keeping out the intense heat of the summer. There were ten such blocks in the barrack area, two of which were for the hospital. There was one wash-house and one latrine for each block. The wash-house, which was twenty yards by covered way from the block, had a central three feet raised brick drained platform, with about twenty taps at one end and four to six cold showers. The latrines were also about twenty yards, by covered way, from the barrack block and consisted of twenty open enclosures with seats - no doors. At the rear of the latrine were trapdoors which permitted the Sweeper (an untouchable) to remove and clean the small round tins placed under the seat. The small tins were emptied by the Sweeper into a large iron, black creosoted tub. This tub was emptied daily into a large tank pulled by a very slow moving Indian buffalo, driven by another untouchable. The troops called the vehicle the 'Bombay Mail' because of its extremely slow movement. You could smell its approach more than two hundred yards away. The furniture in the barrack block consisted of a bed (charpoy) with a tubular metal frame and rope at the base, small wooden box, two wall pegs for equipment and a small stone shelf on the wall for folded greatcoat, spare puttees, mess tin, topee and pith hat. There were no tables or chairs.

On leaving my brother I returned to where I had my bed and found that all my kit had been thrown onto the verandah. I was informed, in no uncertain terms, that corner bed spaces were reserved for older and senior boys. As the boy who had thrown my kit out was six feet tall and coming up to the age of eighteen, I accepted this ruling without argument, but swore to myself that one day I would even the score when the odds were more favourable. However, he gained very little from his bullying manner as the boys were moved later in the day to a double storied building, the only one in the whole barrack area. It contained the library, billiard room, canteen, grocery bar and the Band practice room, and was well segregated from the men. I saw the Taj Mahal for the first time, from the roof of this building - the moon was shining and the Taj looked so serenely beautiful and very peaceful. Before I really had the opportunity to see much of Agra on the 15th April the Boys, together with a Company from the Battalion, were posted on detached duty to Chaubattia, a Hill station in the Himalayas. It was exactly eleven months after my joining the army.

AGRA TO CHAUBATTIA 1932

On the appointed day, 'D' Company and the Boys, eighteen in number and all between the ages of fifteen and eighteen, left Akbar Barracks in full marching order, full pack, greatcoat, haversack and water bottle; the men carried rifles and ammunition. It was hot and dusty, the temperature being between 90 and 100*F in the shade. The dust kicked up by marching feet stuck to one's nostrils and throat, but fortunately it was only about thirty minutes marching to the railway station at Agra Cantonment. A kit-bag with the remainder of my worldly possessions, and a bed roll consisting of two blankets and a dhurrie, had left earlier for the station by AT cart. The Hill Station to which we were posted was Chaubattia, a small outpost about sixty miles from the foot-hill railhead of Kathgodam. 'D' Company was due to stay in Kathgodam for three months, the boys for about six months.

It took about 36 hours to reach the railhead at Kathgodam and proved to be my second slow journey by troop train within a period of three weeks. This time however, I felt that I was amongst friends, boys of my own unit. Two of the boys I knew very well, Martin from Sheffield and Hall from Southampton, who had both been with me in Tidworth. They had left Tidworth about four months earlier than I had and joined the 2nd Battalion in Peshawar. Martin was taken prisoner by the Japanese at the battle at the Sittang River in Burma on the 23rd February 1942. Martin could swim, but his close friend Ansell could not. They were both taken prisoner and spent over three years in Mandalay Jail. They returned to the UK in 1945 with both in good health. It was a slow and very uncomfortable journey since we were packed six to a compartment measuring about 4ft by 6ft 3in for sitting, eating, sleeping and the storage of all our equipment. The distance from Agra to Kathgodam was about 240 miles, passing through the towns of Mathura, Sikandra, Bareilly and Baheri and over the massive bridge spanning the Ganges. I awoke in the early hours of the morning on the 17th April in a stationary train and breathing the cool clean sweet air of the Himalayas, an unbelievable change from the hot dusty air of the plains. The foot hills looked so cool, calm and peaceful and so green with a light bluish haze. With everyone being still asleep I was the only one awake so there was not a sound anywhere. It was a sight and an experience which I have remembered with pleasure all my life. I made many subsequent journeys to the Himalayas but it was this first journey that remains as fresh and vivid in my memory today as it was that morning over eighty years ago. No soldier, however rough and of any sensitivity, who has been to these hills, especially after spending time on the dry burning plains, can deny the Hindu his belief that his Gods abide in these hills.

The whole Company of about one hundred men, plus the boys, travelled the sixty miles from Kathgodam to Chaubattia in a fleet of ambulances, the front and sides of which were canvas covered leaving the only view of the outside world being through the rear of the ambulance. My main recollection of the landscape, as the vehicle twisted and turned, was of steep pine covered hills, enormous bushes of cacti twenty feet tall, the cool sweet air as we moved higher into the hills and the dry-stone walls about eighteen inches high on one side of the road, which offered no protection from certain death if the vehicle went over the side. On this sixty mile journey there must have been at least sixty hair-pin bends, plus difficult corners every few yards with the result that seventy percent of the soldiers were violently sick. It was a great relief to reach our destination and get one's feet onto firm ground. Normally the troops marched from the railhead to the hill-station, but why it had been decided on this occasion that we should travel by ambulance no-one knew. Wayside camps are provided in the Himalayas, located at distances of about twenty odd miles apart, for such moves and are generally located next to stone-strewn rivers with clean cold water running down from the high hills. I did many such marches during the next four years to several different hill-stations.

On alighting from the ambulance, and refreshingly stretching my cramped limbs, I proceeded to collect the remainder of my worldly possessions, kit -bag and bed roll, from the baggage ambulance and then on to my new home for the next five or six months - a long low hut, wood framed with baked mud walls and perched perilously on the side of the hill. It had two doors and eight small windows, a wooden floor and a metal corrugated roof. The apex of the roof was about eight feet high and the sides just over six feet high. It was large enough to accommodate twenty soldiers, allowing an average of about three feet between beds. The furniture consisted of a bed for each person made up of two iron double bed legs, two six feet lengths of corrugated metal fifteen inches wide, two wooden pegs on the wall for one's equipment and a two feet wooden shelf fixed on the wall for folded greatcoat, tope, mess-tin and spare puttees. A small wooden box, which fitted under the bed, two small paraffin oil lamps (quite useless) and one sweeping brush, completed the total furniture. My first duty was to draw three mattress covers and one pillow case from the Quarter Master's store, and proceed to the Company store and fill them. There is quite an art to shredding the coir and filling these covers, at which I eventually became quite efficient, after spending two or three uncomfortable nights on lumpy coir with the possibility of rolling out of bed. Similar huts to ours, sufficient to accommodate the whole Company, were located haphazardly on the hillside wherever the landscape permitted.

Chaubattia is a little over six thousand feet above sea level with a beautiful clear view of the permanent snow covered mountains of the Himalayas. They looked so close, but were in fact about seventy miles away. In every direction, as far as the eye could see, were green pine covered hills. There were three small, bare earthed parade grounds, each the size of a football ground - one for each of the Companies on station. There was no other level ground; it was uphill or downhill everywhere you went. It was a climb to the canteen, a climb to the dining room, downhill three hundred feet to the toilets - quite a feat on a dark night with only the stars to light the way and having a touch of diarrhoea. One night I did not manage it and eased myself halfway down, it was there for everyone to see in the morning - I did not own up. The Sweeper, an untouchable, cleaned it up without complaint or comment.

There was one cinema which had a change of films (talkies) once a week. The seating consisted of tin/wire chairs which could conveniently be moved, if a big head was obstructing your view. Roasted peanuts, wrapped in conical old sheets of newspaper were sold for one anna during the four or five intervals that were needed for the changing of film reels. The price of admittance was eight annas for men and four annas for Boys. A horse stall was located in the centre of the station where a horse could be hired for two hours at a cost of six annas. There were lots of forest paths and rides suitable for would-be learners like me. Normally, four or five boys would hire at the same time and until we had become accustomed to the locality and the horse, one of the owners of the horses would accompany us. They also ensured that we were given an appropriate horse according to our ability to ride. The majority of the horse owners were tall Afghans who were very proud of their horses and meticulously groomed and cared for them. If you hired a horse to go to Raniket, another hill-station about three miles away, the horse was handed over to a relative of the owner at the Raniket stall. On some occasions the owner would hold onto the horse's tail and run all the way to Raniket. If you left Raniket after dark, it was much safer to walk, as the road and path were very narrow, steep in places with sheer drops and no lights. There were also panthers in the vicinity and lots of hyenas and jackals which could frighten the horse.

There were plenty of competitive boxing, football and hockey matches between the three Companies in Chaubattia and also other Companies in Raniket. It was here that I played in my first hockey match, which was not very successful for me as I had been detailed to play in goal and let in six goals. I never played in goal again, but I did learn to love the game and became quite proficient as a Winger or as Centre Half. I was selected to play for the Battalion at the age of seventeen. I continued to play hockey up to the age of 51 years, playing for the army in Burma, Malta and Singapore, for the Service Corps in Europe and for all the units to which I was subsequently posted. The other two units in Chaubattia were a Company from the Cheshire Regiment and a Company from the Highland Light Infantry, together with its bagpipes. For the next three months I heard the unfamiliar whine of the bagpipes drifting over the hills. Thirty two years later, when I was a Captain in the Royal Army Service Corps (RASC) in Taunton, I sat next to a Major General at a Regimental Dinner who had been a 2nd Lieutenant in this Cheshire Company. Quite a small world so we had lots to talk about.

The general routine of the day, Monday to Saturday, except for Thursday which was a free day handed down from the British Raj as a wash day, was Reveille at 6.00am, physical training, boxing and a road run of about two miles. 'Breakfast at 7.45 am, Bugle or Band instrument instruction at 9.00 am, Dinner at 12.45pm and Education from 2.00 to 4.00pm. (I sat for my Second Class Certificate of Education and successfully passed it). Tea was at 4.15pm and the Boys were also given Supper at 7.00pm, which normally consisted of a meat sandwich or bread and jam and a mug of cocoa. Once a fortnight there was a route march or a 'dog and stick', the latter being done under your own steam with various reporting points to ensure you did the full distance. There was a Company Drill Parade once a week, normally before breakfast. After Tea, the rest of the day was your own. There were several government orchards in the vicinity of Chaubattia on which the Boys did military styled raids; an initial reconnaissance, placement of sentries, an elite snatch (procurement) party and a rear guard to put any pursuers off the scent. We were always successful and were never caught.

I experienced my first 'short arm inspection', after about a fortnight in Chaubattia. It was held on the Parade Ground in full view of anyone on the road. The Medical Officer (MO) sat in a chair and as you marched up to him you dropped your KD shorts, (the top half of your body being already bare), and raised your arms above your head. The MO was looking for VD, Crabs and Ringworms. If there was any sign of wetness on the penis, he pulled and squeezed it, and if he thought it necessary, you were sent to the Medical Centre for a smear to be taken. I marched boldly up to the chair when it came to my turn and dropped my shorts, but before I had chance to raise my arms, he motioned me to pass on, saying, "I don't have time to look for it". I did not know whether to feel angry, insulted or ashamed.

For the next few months, I took an awful lot of stick from the older Boys.

On the whole, I enjoyed my stay in Chaubattia. I was initially bullied by some of the bigger and older Boys, but on fighting back a few times, although I always got the worst of it, my oppressors eventually transferred their attention to someone else. On one occasion, after I had been found guilty by a 'Barrack-room Court Martial', for not sweeping the room satisfactorily, I was sentenced to run one hundred yards up the road with rifle and full equipment, my pack being filled with stones. My friend, Martin, helped me on with the pack, it being too heavy for me to lift by myself, but when he let go, I fell backwards onto my backside - to the merriment of everyone watching. I was determined to do the one hundred yards and showed my oppressors they could not hurt or break me. I vowed that one day I would even the score. It was on occasions such as these that my engagement for four years Boy service, nine years Man service and three years on the Reserves, seemed to stretch into an eternity. The food was very plain, but plentiful and as I was always hungry and growing I generally left a clean plate. I received three rupees pay every Friday which saw me through the whole week. I was quite careful with my money, never borrowing or going into debt. Fruit, such as oranges, apples, apricots, pineapples and mangoes were extremely cheap and although I ate lots of these, it made little headway into my three rupees. To relieve my gnawing hunger between breakfast and dinner, I lavishly expended two annas every morning on a mug of tea and a hefty piece of cake from the Char Wallah who, regular as clockwork, came to the bungalow with his tea urn and box of cakes at 10.30am.

I bought a small paraffin lamp for eight annas to enable me to read at night, the two lamps officially provided barely lit up the room sufficiently to see one's way around. I also bought a battery torch for use if ever I had to find my way down the hill to the toilets in an emergency late at night. I had, of course, to buy boot polish, metal polish, toothpaste, soap and white and green blanco. In addition, there was the upkeep of my clothing, but for this we were credited with a monthly clothing allowance which, if one was careful, adequately covered all necessary replacements. The most troublesome aspect of life in Chaubattia was the heavy infestation of bed bugs, a smelly blood sucking bug about one fifth of an inch in size when empty but considerably larger when full of blood. They lived in the cracks of the mud walls and in the crevices of the two metal bed pieces and came out at night in their hundreds to feed. If one was on your pillow, a foot from your nose, you could smell the foul thing. Two or three times each week we disassembled the bed, held the six feet pieces upright and thumped them on the floor. As the bugs dropped off we squashed them with our PT shoes. Once every two or three months, we immersed the two metal pieces in a tank of boiling water treated with a disinfectant. The bites from the bugs, though not a serious problem, often turned septic and looked disgustingly dirty.

One morning just after Reveille a boy by the name of Whitfield, six feet tall broadly built and coming up to the age of eighteen, came up to the CO in charge, and said "Corp, look at what the bloody bugs have done to me". He dropped his shorts and showed the Corporal his dangly bits - I got a full view as my bed was next to the NCO's. His testicles were the size of tennis balls and his penis had the appearance of a section of a bicycle inner tube. He could barely see from his extremely swollen and puffy eyes. He reported to the Medical Officer and was admitted to hospital. After two or three weeks in hospital his condition was diagnosed as inherited syphilis, aggravated by bug bites. After discharge from hospital he carried on with normal duties, but had to report for treatment - a needle, every Saturday morning. He was still continuing this treatment up to the outbreak of war with Japan in 1941; he did however manage to infect himself, by his own efforts, with syphilis in 1937.

It was in Chaubattia, where I saw my first dead black panther. It was shot by a Lance Corporal using a Mannlicher rifle. The bullet had entered the front of the body and exited breaking a back leg and the tail. It was a massive and beautiful beast, with a skin smoother than black velvet. 'D' Company was relieved by 'B' Company in late June, it being the aim of the military to give all troops stationed on the plains, where possible, a tour of three months in the hills during the hot season, at least every two to three years. This was an absolute necessity on health grounds and most definitely paid dividends in keeping the army fit and healthy. Prior to one of these changeovers the Boys moved into a smaller bungalow. When eight of the Boys had attained the age of eighteen they were posted to man service, and I was glad to see some of them go. The new bungalow was nearer to the washrooms and the toilets - I dreaded dark nights and loose bowels.

In 'B' Company there was a Sergeant by the name of Calvert who came from the Doncaster area. While serving with 5th KOYLI during World War One he had been awarded the Victoria Cross for his bravery at the second Battle of Havrincourt - 11 September 1918. His citation stated that he had, single handed, attacked a German machine gun post and shot and bayoneted the gunners and by doing so had saved many of his comrades lives. We, the Boys, had found a live hero to worship. We took every opportunity to talk with him. He liked his beer, and on many occasions had too much. Any misdemeanour on his part never went any further than the Company Commander. 'B' Company and the Boys returned to Agra in mid October; the six months that I had spent in Chaubattia had passed quite quickly and had been a new and interesting experience. On arrival in Agra I could not help observing the marked difference between the troops returning from the hills and those who had spent the summer on the plains. The latter were pale, lethargic and looked drained of energy, whilst those from the hills were sun-tanned and full of life and vigour.

In October, I began studying for my 1st Class Certificate of Education, three hours in the morning and two hours in the afternoon. The class consisted of one other Boy (Steermint), five or six Sergeants, two acting CSM's and one Private soldier by the name of Metcalfe. Steermint and I took the full five subjects involved and the others took three or fewer subjects, depending on the amount of time they could devote to education from their other duties. Steermint and I were excused all other duties and were therefore able to attend full time. The teacher was a tall and thin Warrant Officer from the Education Corps with several War medals and considerable service in the army. He was a good and well-liked soldier and Steermint and I soon found out that he was a strong disciplinarian. We received many a clip on the ear for inattention - looking back, perhaps they were quite justified. As fifteen year olds, unlike the men who required the necessary certificates for promotion, we did not take education too seriously and often found it a little irksome. After about six months of daily education we took the examination on 23rd March 1933. Both Steermint and I were successful, passing in all subjects. The remainder of the class had various passes and failures. My time was now to be devoted to normal duties and musical studies.

Agra, famous for its beautiful Taj Mahal is about one hundred and thirty miles south east of Delhi, in the middle of plains stretching miles across India. Winter is from October to late February, fairly warm and dry but cool after sundown. Khaki Serge is worn after sundown in December and January. Summer, April to September, is very hot reaching 120*F in the shade. The refreshing cool Monsoon is very welcome in June and July. Agra could be said to consist of a city, a town and a Cantonment. The City, densely populated, had narrow and dirty streets, open sewers, lots of rats and thick with flies. Many of the houses were mud built, some wood built and some of brick. The majority had flat roofs. Canvas and rusty metal lean-to shacks were erected anywhere and everywhere. Indian bullocks wandered unhindered in the streets. The town, about a mile and a half from the Cantonment, had wide well maintained streets. The population in general consisted of retired European Businessmen, retired British Civil Servants, a considerable number of Anglo-Indians - mainly officials from the Railways, and well-to-do higher caste Indians. The bungalows they lived in were well built with spacious well maintained gardens. The latter rarely mixed with British Officers or with British troops. There were two cinemas in town, the Palace and the Empire. Both showed English films four times a week, on the other three days they showed Indian films. Both had switched from 'Silent' to 'Talkies', a few weeks prior to the Battalion arriving from Peshawar in April. A ticket to the cinema cost me, as a Boy, four annas - the cost for a soldier was eight annas. At sunset the flower gardens and paths surrounding the cinema were sprayed with water by a Bhisti using a goat's skin, which provided a cool and pleasant atmosphere.

The Cantonment, Akbar Barracks, which the KOYLI occupied, was about one and a half miles from the town. The total military strength of British troops in Agra, was one Battalion of Infantry, one Battery of Artillery, plus small numbers of personnel of Royal Army Medical Corps (RAMC), Ordinance and Signals. Akbar Barracks was well spread out, having it's own hospital, a 600 yard firing range, Hockey, Football and Rugby grounds and Tennis and Squash Courts. The Rugby ground celebrated the only green grass in the Cantonment. There was a Wet and Dry canteen for Other Ranks, an Officer's and Sergeant's Mess, a separate Dining room for each of the five Companies of the Battalion, a library and a Billiard room. There were official contracts for local Tailors, Cobblers, Barbers and Cycle stands. A bicycle could be hired for four annas a week, which included all repairs and if necessary a replacement. About two hundred yards from the Barracks were five or six married quarters, for the married personnel of the Battalion. There were few married soldiers at this time as the age limit to be on the married list was 26 years of age. There was one very small indoor swimming pool, in a converted windowless building about twenty feet by twenty feet and four feet deep where I taught myself to swim. The Garrison Church, St George's, could accommodate up to about a thousand personnel. On normal Sunday's about 400 troops, the married families and a handful of civilians attended. On festival days such as Easter and Christmas, the church was packed to capacity - large numbers of Anglo-Indians attending. I dreaded the weekly Church parade. I was in the Band and stood in the sun, mostly at attention, for up to one hour prior to the Battalion actually moving off to the church. The Band was initially inspected by the RSM, followed by inspection by the Adjutant prior to the Companies taking up their positions on the parade ground - which took about thirty minutes. The dress was Khaki drill jackets and slacks. The jacket was buttoned right up to the neck and was stiff with starch and uncomfortable, which was the main cause of many of the soldiers fainting. In summer the temperature went up to 120*F in the shade. I fainted on many occasions. It was customary to leave you where you fell until you regained consciousness and resumed your position in the ranks. The soldiers in the Companies were armed with rifles and bayonets, with one Company also having twenty rounds of live ammunition. A precaution observed since the Indian Mutiny of 1857 when unarmed soldiers in church were taken by surprise by armed mutineers. Now slots were provided in the pews for the rifles. During the service many of the troops fell asleep, but amazingly woke up immediately the parson intoned, "Now to God the Father..."

A daily routine, which commenced an hour before Reveille, was that the barber (Nappy) who would quietly pull the mosquito net aside and shave the occupant whilst he was still asleep. His equipment consisted of a small brass canister holding considerably less than a pint of water, with a charcoal heater underneath, a brush, a lump of soap, a small towel and a cut-throat razor. His charge was four annas a week. He shaved about forty men every morning, using the same brush, water and towel - not very hygienic. As I did not start shaving until well after the Battalion left Agra in March 1936, I never partook of his service.

All troops were expected to take part in some type of sport or exercise every evening after sun-down. There were also excellent opportunities for shooting deer, black buck and wild pig. A variety of guns and rifles were available from the Armoury free of charge, the ammunition used being charged to one's account (on the slate) so, when out of funds you could still go shooting. From 1933, at the age of sixteen and up to leaving Agra in 1936, I went shooting on many occasions with a .22 rifle. I shot at practically anything that moved in the air or on the ground; sparrows; pigeons, kite-hawks, vultures (which were a protected bird), pariah dogs, deer and snakes. I was of 'marksman' standard with the .303 rifle and was also in the 'All India Young Soldiers (under 18 years) Rifle team. Although the Battalion was very fit and healthy and the majority of the troops being under the age of twenty-five, there was still a considerable number of deaths from disease, such as malaria, cholera, typhus, rabies, heat-stroke and from accidents and suicides. Burials were quickly arranged and it was possible to have dinner with someone and then attend his funeral in the evening. There was one very sad case of a Lance Corporal (L/Cpl) in the Buglers (HQ Company) being very depressed as several of his friends had just completed their overseas tour of six/seven years and had left for the UK. In the early morning on the day after his friends had left he ran amok with a ceremonial Gurkha kukri and severely injured a number of soldiers before cutting his own throat in the adjoining wash-house. His head was almost severed with blood splashed six feet up the wall. I saw his body placed on a table top and carried by four men to the hospital. One of those he most severely injured was a Bugler, Megson who required a great number of stitches in his back. It was a miracle that no one was killed. Fortunately, all the injured recovered. The band, as usual, led the funeral party, (a platoon of about thirty men), in the evening. Prior to moving off from the mortuary, the coffin was opened for those wishing to bid a last farewell. Being curious, but I don't think morbid, I ventured a look into the coffin. The surgeon had not done a very good job of stitching up the wound and had left him with a horrible snarl on his face. He was buried in the Military Cemetery, an old, isolated and grim Victorian one about a mile from the Barracks and on the way to the cinemas in town. The Band played slow solemn music, 'Dead March from Saul', all the way to the cemetery. After the padre had completed the graveside service and the firing party had fired off a volley of blanks, all of which took about ten minutes, we were on our way back to barracks playing cheerful and popular marches at the speed of 132 paces to the minute. Whenever I was returning from the cinema on a dark night, I passed this isolated and grim reminder of the dead as quickly as possible; I could still see that snarl. The kit of a soldier who died was put up for auction. His Company colleagues competed with each other to purchase some memento, especially his leather ammunition pouches and polished boots. Many items, such as socks, towels, puttees and items of khaki drill were bought and then put back up for re-auction, which meant that these items were sold and bought several times. All bids were debited to one's account; the money raised was forwarded to the next of kin in the UK.

The normal route marches in Agra were of about twenty miles on extremely dusty country roads and tracks, through small rural villages in and around Agra. A common site was to see women slapping cow dung mixed with cut straw into flat cakes and putting them onto the walls of the house to dry. These were used for fuel. One soldier newly arrived from England, a bandsman by the name of Cox, of doubtful intellect, a pipe smoker and subject to epileptic fits, was told during one of these marches that the cakes were made of tobacco leaf. He slyly slid one of the cakes, during a halt, into his web pack and took it back to Barracks where he soon realised it was not for smoking. Four years later in Burma he was discharged on medical grounds. Everyone in the Band knew he was half crazy and subject to lots of fits, and why it had taken the army authorities four years to find this out was a mystery. It was generally understood that the only bar to being accepted into the military was to have flat feet. In summer it was very hot on these marches and one perspired enormously.

On completion of the march there was scarcely a dry patch anywhere on one's uniform. I remember on one occasion when sweat from my head passed completely through my one inch pith-hat. On another occasion, on returning to Barracks, I squeezed out almost a half pint of sweat from my socks.

Once a year, the Battalion, in full strength, marched through the city of Agra. It was a tradition of the Raj and was a form of 'showing the flag'. The city was densely populated and much more interesting than the usual monotonous marches through open country. Everyone appeared to be friendly and interested in the troops, especially the children who ran alongside asking for 'buckshees'. Even the lowest paid soldier could afford to give the odd anna (1d) to such happy looking children. The anna is made up of four paisa, and each paisa is made up of three pies.

Note (added).....

- 1 Rupee=16 Anna
- 1 Anna = 4 paisa
- 1 Paisa = 3 pies
- Hence 1 Rupee = 16 Annas, 64 paisa or 192 pies.

Whatever was given was received with such genuine gratitude and pleasure, that the soldier actually got real satisfaction from the giving.

At Christmas 1932 the sixteen boys, all between the ages of fifteen and eighteen, were invited to the Married Families (Civilian and Military) Christmas party which was held in the gymnasium. Father Christmas arrived on an elephant to the great enjoyment of the children. An Indian snake charmer with a basket full of evil looking snakes was followed by a juggler who provided interesting entertainment. However, the Boy soldiers were more interested in the food, disposing of enormous quantities of cakes, buns and trifles. I heard one of the wives serving the food say, "They shouldn't need anything more to eat until next Christmas".

The Battalion had three days free from all duties, except for the men detailed for guard and picket duties. In accordance with tradition, the Warrant Officers and senior NCO served up the Christmas dinner to the troops - with considerable humour and controlled banter. There was plenty of goose, with all the appropriate trimmings, and lavish portions of Christmas pudding. The men each received a pint bottle of beer, not withstanding that most of them were already drunk and stayed that way for the rest of the Christmas break.

My brother James received a Christmas cake from my brother Charles and sister-in-law Alice in England and, being on the top rate of pay of three shillings a day, paid the necessary postal dues. I was still on one shilling a day. He gave me half the cake, which I shared with my close friends. It was unusual for anyone to receive a parcel from England, even at Christmas. Charles and Alice kindly sent another cake for Christmas in 1933, which arrived in early January. James again paid the postal dues and, as my brother Sidney had joined us, having spent Christmas day on the train journeying from Bombay, the cake was divided into three; my share was getting smaller. Although the cake had taken over four weeks to reach Agra, it was in very good condition and tasted extremely good. I asked Sidney why he had an extremely short hair cut and he told me that he had spent several days under close arrest on the troopship.

I looked forward to all meals at this time since I was always hungry and at last I had started to grow. My favourite meal was breakfast which consisted of porridge, tasty pork or beef rissoles, bread and tea. My brother James bought a small packet of butter from the dairy vendor every morning, for two annas, and gave me half. Breakfast could be supplemented very cheaply from the vendors plying their trade on the outer veranda. They provided fried or boiled duck and chicken eggs, bacon, ham and toast; I preferred the duck eggs as they were bigger and also cheaper. For dinner we had roast beef or stew, a chapatti (at least 260 times a year), potatoes and a vegetable, followed by rice pudding or prunes and custard. On some occasions we had fresh fruit, generally mangoes or water melon. Tea consisted of two slices of bread with margarine and jam.

Again, it was possible to supplement this from the vendors on the veranda. Supper for the Boys was normally a plate of left over stew and a slice of bread or a rissole sandwich. There was no such thing as cold water in summer as it came out of the cold taps quite hot. Before the monsoon broke, the dust around the Barrack blocks, and on the roadsides, was several inches deep; like very fine hot sand. Within an hour of the monsoon breaking, the sand was covered by several inches of water. The troops rushed out of the Barrack rooms, completely naked, and frolicked in the torrential downpour. It cured the prickly heat (red itchy spots) instantly, and brought the temperature down most dramatically.

Parades in summer commenced at 6.00am and ended about 10.00am, with the exception of route marches, guards, pickets and church parades. Where necessary they would start again at 6.00pm. The Battalion was very smart and efficient with its weapons and was very well drilled. A CO's, Adjutant's or RSM's drill parade was held weekly. The smartness was helped by the fact that the khaki drill uniform was cheap and that the jackets, slacks and shorts could be quickly washed and ironed for the small sum of one anna per garment, by the 'flying dhobi'. The official free washing contract dhobi came twice a week, the flying dhobi once every day. The Battalion "Trooped the Colour" on the 2nd February 1934. This was an important, but seldom carried out parade, which the majority of soldiers on seven year engagements rarely experienced. To ensure near perfection, practice parades were carried out with monotonous regularity, months before the actual parade. The Viceroy of India at this time, and the virtual ruler of 400 million people, was Lord Willingdon who took the salute. For the Viceroy to visit an individual unit was a most unusual occurrence. He arrived by plane on the Miadam, adjacent to the old Victorian Cantonment Cemetery, possibly the first plane to land or be seen in Agra. The Colonel of the Regiment, Lieutenant General C.P. Deeds, came all the way from England for the occasion, again unusual as the normal travelling time from England was over three weeks. All troops taking part in the parade were ordered to purchase a new suit of khaki drill, which made quite a hole in one's clothing allowance. The complicated drill movements, the fixing and unfixing of bayonets, and the march past the saluting base were carried out with meticulous precision and smartness was a marvellous picture that remains vividly in my memory. On the completion of the parade a special dinner, a free pint bottle of beer (if being a Boy you could sneak one - most Boys did) and the remainder of the day was declared a holiday, which made up to some degree for the many monotonous rehearsals that we had endured.

I was now a 'Boy Bandsman' having passed all the necessary examinations required in respect of the clarinet and general musical knowledge expected of a Bandsman. My pay was increased from 1s (5d) per day to 1s 2d per day. The Band Master, J.C.J. Martin, never let me forget this enormous increase to my pay. Whenever I made a wrong note, or misread the key signature, he would make a nasty caustic remark regarding my worthiness of being awarded the princely sum of 2d. There were several occasions when I felt like informing him that he could take the 2d back and put it in a safe and personal depository.

On the 31st May 1934, the Battalion had just been dismissed from a routine parade when I felt something like a touch of dizziness; it was the Quetta earthquake in the north of India over 700 miles away in which over 20,000 people died. In the same year, the Battalion proceeded by train to Delhi to take part in six weeks of Brigade, Divisional and Corps training. British, Indian and Gurkha troops were taking part. Our accommodation in Delhi consisted of 180 lb tents - eight men to a tent, together with our bedding of two blankets and a 1914/18 rubberised cape/groundsheet, full web equipment, rifle and kit-bag. A paraffin hurricane lantern gave us light at night. A type of white ant was quite a nuisance, if you were not vigilant and checked your kit every day it ate holes in the rubberised groundsheet and created havoc in the kit-bag.

For six long and endless weeks we tramped the hot and dusty plains around Delhi, most of the time not knowing what we were supposed to be doing since we were rarely 'put in the picture'. The night operations, wandering about in the dark, sweating one minute on the move and then shivering when stationary for long periods, plus not knowing what it was all about, ensured that the troops took little interest in the exercise. The main interest was getting back to the comfort of camp as quickly as possible. There was no river or stream near the camp, which meant that all washing and bathing was done from a small canvas bucket - one per tent. Water was drawn from water tanks fixed on bullock carts, some hundred yards from the tents. Whoever drew the first bucket of water at Reveille had a good clean wash; the lazy used the same water until it became a discoloured mess in the bottom of the bucket when it had, of necessity, to be replenished. Whenever possible you had a full wash-down using the whole bucket of water. The Band had several breaks from the monotonous military exercise to take part in government ceremonial occasions, church parades and various musical engagements. One such engagement was a Government House cocktail party given by the Viceroy of India. High ranking government and military officials, bedecked and dripping with medals and awards together with their extravagantly dressed ladies mingled with similar medalled Indian Princes and Rajahs together with their ladies and daughters in extraordinary beautiful silk saris. As they arrived all were announced by a tall, bearded military Rajput Toastmaster who announced their rank, names and decorations, which made a very impressive and memorable occasion. We (KOYLI Band) played soft background music from an overhead balcony, with a full view of the proceedings taking place below. When the party ended and all the guests had left, the band sat down to a good supper with unlimited drinks.

Another memorable occasion was an open-air concert given by the massed Bands of India, Gurkha and British Bands drawn from all over India, speaking different languages but all able to read and play the same musical scores. On my stand, repiano clarinet, were a Gurkha and two Gujarati bandsmen. We had difficulty conversing, but musically everything went very well. The concert ended with the massed bands playing the Evening Hymn followed by the Last Post and Reveille. Massed Buglers positioned on the city walls, a considerable distance away, played a synchronised echo to the Last Post and Reveille - a moving and impressive occasion. Our last big engagement was a review of British, Indian and Gurkha troops, all with their own military bands. The mounted Rajputs were especially outstanding smart and colourful with a magnificent military bearing, inherited from their forbearers who were renowned for their valour from and before Mughal times. Other Indian troops consisted of Jats, Baluches, Bengalis, Punjabis, Sikhs, Mahrattas, Gujaratis and many others.

There were many proud, dedicated and well disciplined Indian regiments in the British Army in the 1930's. At one period there were 190,000 Indian troops made up of 100 Infantry Battalions, 21 Cavalry Regiments and 18 Mounted Artillery Batteries. The great majority of these Regiments had been loyal to the British crown during the mutiny of 1856-7. It is a regrettable fact that the British soldier, in my day, was not fully aware, or took the trouble to find out, the true facts of the Mutiny and wrongfully considered that all Indian troops, except the Gurkhas, had mutinied. Forty years after the Mutiny, large numbers of them, loyally and bravely, lost their lives during the Afghan, Sikh, Burma and Middle East wars in the service of the British crown. Later, in the 1914/18 war they fought alongside British troops in extremely difficult and unaccustomed conditions, far different from their own warm and sunny climate; many lost their lives in the 1914/18 war.

The Battalion was very fit but tired after six weeks of monotonous and strenuous training. It was looking forward to returning by train to the comfort of Barracks in Agra. It was quite a surprise to everyone when the news leaked out that the Battalion would march the 120 miles back to Agra. It was understood by the troops that the Commanding Officer had volunteered to do this, to show off the Battalion and to gain credit, career wise. He was well known to never march, except on horseback. Everyone was familiar with his shout at the commencement of a march of, "Scyce gorrah louh"..(Horseman bring me my horse)

It rained the whole of the first day's march and as we had no capes, we were wet through to the skin from morning to night. In accordance with Regulations, we marched for fifty minutes and halted for ten, every hour. The ten minutes was to allow one to adjust cumbersome equipment, relieve oneself, have a smoke and adjust one's puttees. If you had your puttees too tight, they stopped the circulation of blood in your legs, if too slack, they dropped onto your ankles. As we passed through small rural villages with their mud walled dwellings, with countless moth-eaten pariah dogs, laughing naked children, boys and girls, ran alongside the column asking for 'buckshees'. The sound of our Band and Buglers apparently heralded our arrival. It looked as if every villager turned out to see us. The women were heavily veiled, only their eyes showing, not even their feet. It was apparent that the majority of villagers had never seen a military Band and white soldiers; they were very friendly and smiling. Passing through these very isolated villages broke the monotony of an otherwise dreary march. We continually passed and overtook, heavily laden, slow moving bullock carts, some with a live cargo of chattering women and children, others heavily laden with a variety of produce. The drivers appeared to be constantly prodding the beast's backsides with his stick and twisting their tails, to keep them on the move. After about eight hours of marching, we arrived at our first night's camp site, wet and hungry.

The Quarter Master's advance party, including cooks and sanitary personnel, had arrived at the camp some hours earlier and marked out the Company lines, dug out the latrines and prepared a meal. The first duty to be performed was a foot inspection carried out by platoon sergeants. Blisters were numerous on this first day's march as a result of marching on metalled roads; the previous six weeks had been spent on marching over paddy fields and Maidams. All blister had to be punctured and a piece of skin cut out and the feet soaked in potassium permanganate, which though painful, hardened the skin for the next day's march. Tents (180 lbs) were collected from the bullock carts and pitched in meticulously straight lines, each tent accommodating ten men, giving each man a space of about 18 inches by six feet for himself and his equipment. After a visit to the latrines and a quick dip in the nearby river, I felt very refreshed and ready for a good meal. The combined dinner and tea consisted of a plate of stew, a chapatti, a mug of tea and two slices of bread. After collecting our bed-rolls from the bullock carts, which consisted of a groundsheet and two blankets - one's pack made a good pillow, the rest of the day was free, unless you had been detailed for guard or picket. Wet uniforms were a problem - not quite dry when put on the following day. The latrines are worthy of a little more detail. They were prepared prior to the Battalion's arrival by a Lance/Corporal Foster of the Pioneer Section. There was no official layout, it being left to the sadistic caprice of Foster, an old soldier with many years service in India, and considered to be suffering from 'a touch of the sun'.. deolali. One of his duties, when in Barracks, was the construction of coffins for the Battalion and for a few civilians with any army background living in the Agra area. He boasted he always made the corpse fit the coffin, no matter what the size of the body. He took a fiendish delight in taking gruesome photographs of the dead, especially the suicides and for which he found a ready market. He also took the part of the dead and was photographed as such, taking the part of Dracula. I digress, but it is to show the character of the architect of the latrines. The only stipulation regarding the construction was that the trench should be at least two feet deep, surrounded by a canvas screen four feet high, a yellow flag and ample quantities of 'Army form blank'. His general construction was of two parallel trenches about thirty feet long and eight feet apart, with a bamboo pole when obtainable to rest your backside on. On some occasions the pole erected about a foot in front of the trench, which meant you had to grip the pole with your hands and hang your backside over the trench. On other occasions the pole was placed on the very edge of the trench, which necessitated a skilful balancing act. His favourite construction, however, was that which ensured that half of those present, faced the other half's backsides.

Reveille was sounded by the Bugler at 6.00am. Bedding rolls were quickly packed up and taken to the waiting bullock carts. A quick wash in the nearby river was very refreshing. Camps were invariably located, where possible, near a river, canal or lake. Often, many of the soldiers who were too lazy to go down to the river to wash and shave after breakfast used a portion of their tea for this purpose. The tents were emptied of all equipment and all but two of the guide ropes loosened and all tent pegs pulled out of the ground. The two remaining ropes, holding up the tent, were held by two men. On the sounding of a 'G' by the Bugler, fifty to sixty tents were dropped in uniform, folded up and carried at the double to the waiting bullock carts that were already harnessed up to move off to the next camp site. Breakfast consisted of two slices of bread, bacon, an egg fried two hours earlier and a mug of tea. After breakfast, fatigue parties dusted the latrines with lime and filled them in with the previously removed earth. Lines of men moved slowly through the camping area, picking up every scrap of paper, cigarette packs etc. When the Battalion finally moved out, the camp site was left spotlessly clean with practically no sign that over 600 men had just spent the night there. The same procedure was repeated at five more camp sites prior to our arrival in Agra. During our stay in Delhi, a new draft of soldiers from England had arrived in Agra and with them was my younger brother, David. I was extremely surprised to see him as I had no idea that he had enlisted; mail from England was extremely rare and took four weeks to reach India. He was not quite sixteen years of age and looked very pale compared to myself, having spent six weeks in the open air. A few days later he was sick with dysentery, having eaten unwashed fruit, and spent a week or so in hospital. There were now four Price brothers serving in the KOYLI in Agra.

AGRA – CHAUBATTIA 1934

I was rapidly becoming an old 'boy soldier' of nearly seventeen years of age. I and my friend Moules, who came from Leeds, proceeded to the Barra bazaar in town with the intention of procuring for ourselves a forbidden bottle of something to celebrate Christmas. Army regulations allowed beer only, no wines or spirits to be consumed by soldiers (OR's) and Boys, nothing stronger than lemonade. After considerable discussion and haggling with the owner of the wine store, we eventually purchased a bottle of Vermouth. We had not the slightest idea of the potency of the contents but we liked the look of the label and the price suited our pocket. We camouflaged our purchase in a shoe box and carefully taking it in turn, carried it back to Barracks. On arrival in our Barrack room, we meticulously divided the contents into out two chipped enamel mugs, cleaned for this special occasion. We did not particularly like the taste but did not admit this to our many envious colleagues. We drank it much too quickly, with the result that we both felt a little sick and considerably tipsy; nevertheless, we considered that we had 'proved' our manhood. The NCO in-charge of Boys, L/Cpl Clark, an old soldier of 1914/18 vintage, who on occasions had been known to drink a bucket full of beer, on hearing of our booze-up, admonished us, but with a slight twinkle in his eye. I think he considered it a further necessary step in our education. My friend Moules was later killed at the battle on the river Sittang by Japanese rifle fire, whilst endeavouring to rescue a wounded comrade.

No Christmas cake from England. Charles and Alice probably considered it not worthwhile as there were now four of the family serving in Agra, James, Sidney, myself and David. The Army Boys were again invited to the Married families Children's Christmas party and did justice to the well laid table of dainty sandwiches, cakes, buns, trifles etc. Father Christmas arrived, with his bulky bags of gifts, on a camel - he did ring the changes on his mode of arrival; one year an elephant, the next a bullock cart and this year a camel. The young children from the married families were ecstatic in their welcome of Father Christmas, but I don't think any of them queried why the camel and not the reindeers. This was my last attendance to this party as I was due to move onto man service on the 23rd February 1935.

A few days before Christmas, the Army Boys had another party. Major T.A.B. Butt's wife gave a party for the boys in the grounds of their bungalow. We had a large variety of party games, with prizes for the winners and lots to eat and drink, but no alcohol. We were very careful to be on our best behaviour as the Major was a stern looking person whom we rarely came into contact with. With his stern military visage and rows of 1914-18 war medals, he was almost a god in our eyes. Looking back, I think Mrs Butt herself personally enjoyed the party and the company of the Boys; she had no children of her own. It was rumoured, that a few years earlier, they had considered adopting one of the Army (orphan) boys. It was generally understood in the Battalion that their failure to have a family was the result of the Major having one of his testicles shot off in the 1914-18 war. Major Butt took over command of the Battalion a few months later in September 1935 and was promoted to Lt Colonel.

On 23rd February 1935, I attained the age of eighteen years and thus moved onto man service, acquiring the princely sum of 2s 3d per day. This was my maximum entitlement not withstanding that I had passed all my musical, military and educational requirements. It would be raised to 2s 9d on my nineteenth birthday and to 3s 0d on my 21st birthday, if I continued to pass my annual rifle shooting, judging distance tests and also kept myself free from VD. I had no qualms on qualifying as I had been a marksman with the rifle from the age of sixteen and as yet, women were totally unknown to me; I was still a virgin soldier and the thought of VD, the punishment and the treatment, frightened me to death.

A small break from the routine of military life occurred when riots between Muslims and Hindus, broke out in the city of Agra resulting in serious fires and looting on a grand scale. The Battalion was called out by the civilian authorities to assist in the maintenance of law and order. Fires were burning everywhere and smoke overhung the city and there were large numbers of belligerent looters and arsonists. The situation was quite serious and at one point I split the butt of my rifle, which was brass plated, on the head of a looter. Law and order was eventually restored without the necessity of using live ammunition. I got a new rifle.

Christmas 1935, my fourth in Agra. Christmas was always looked forward to with considerable anticipation, not necessarily for its religious significance but because of the one break in the year from the strict military life, a change of diet for at least one day and the two or three days free from parades, training, barrack room inspections and no Reveille. I volunteered to act as Mess Orderly on Christmas day together with my friend Moules. We had both moved onto man service earlier in the year. The dinner was served in accordance with KOYLI tradition, by the Band-Master, Bugle Major, CSM, CQMS and Sergeants of HQ Company. They took polite but barbed criticism regarding their serving abilities, in the right spirit. Everyone was relaxed and friendly. The dinner consisted of large portions of goose, roast and boiled potatoes, a variety of vegetables and a good helping of Xmas pudding and custard; washed down with a pint bottle of beer. As approximately half the men were drunk and incapable of movement well before the dinner, there were large quantities of beer and pudding left over. Moules and I took the surplus pudding, about twenty pounds, which just fitted into our barrack room boxes. We ate it every day for the next two weeks. The surplus beer was taken by two of the older volunteers. Three months later, in March 1936, there was a rumour that we were going to either China or Burma. The rumour was over when it was confirmed that the Battalion was bound for Maymyo in Upper Burma.

FLP 4688132 KOYLI 1931. Xmas leave December 1931

On the way to Bombay, India. 4th March 1932, HMT Nevasa

Agra 1932. FLP (Bandboy) 4688132 KOYLI

4688132 Boy FL PRICE 2nd KOYLI, Agra, India 1932

Agra 1932-6 Water Well & Barrack Room

Agra India 1932-6 Typical Barrack Block. (Seven of these Blocks accommodated the full Bn.

Barrack Room Agra 1932. Air circulated by Punkhas

1932 4 KOYLI soldiers on a 'Dog & Stick'
in the Himalayas near Chaubattia, India

Resting on Mountain road near Rannikhet
(Pakistan) 1932

North western Frontier, India 1932. Two soldiers and mules of 2nd KOYLI

Chakrata India 1933. FLP 4th from Left,,Middle row L to R; Clark, Tidswell, Moulds, Menton, Farr, Kemp, Judd, Boot, Martin, FLP, Hall, Wishart

2nd Bn KOYLI. On the road to Chakrata, India 1933

Fatepur Sikri Camp near Agra. 2nd Bn KOYLI 1933-5

Agra Railway Station 1933

Chakrata (India) 1933-4. Dog & Stick 2nd KOYLI

Agra 1933 Boys of HQ Company KOYLI. FLP head on left of pillar

2nd Feb 1934 - March Past 2nd Bn KOYLI (Trooping the Colour)- Viceroy (Lord Willingdon) attended, a rare occasion. Lt Gen C.P. Deeds (Col. of the Reg) also attended. Jim, Sid and Fred Price on parade.

Agra India 2nd Feb 1934. Viceroy's Plane on Agra landing ground.

The Viceroys Plane. 16 years later I met the pilot in Aldershot.
2 Feb 1934 Agra, India

AGRA TO BURMA – MARCH 1936

The 2nd Battalion KOYLI was relived from duty by a Battalion of the Welsh Regiment in March 1936. Our last night in Agra was spent on the verandas of the Barrack rooms; we had no beds, just a dhurrie and two blankets, the beds being used by the Welsh. Everyone had been looking forward to the move as four years in Agra had been quite a strain, mainly because of the extremely hot weather, no female company, very little live entertainment and the monotonous year in, year out of basic military life. I had many very pleasant memories of my life in Agra but the thought of the cool green of Upper Burma was very refreshing. I had studied details of the history, peoples, products, climate and the annexation of Burma when studying for my First Class Certificate of Education in 1933. I was personally looking forward to this change of scenery with great interest and anticipation.

Several days had been taken up in packing the Battalion's heavy baggage, the Printers and Armourers shops having the heaviest and most cumbersome equipment. Fatigues in respect of these were therefore avoided whenever possible. These last days in Agra were sweaty and exhaustive but, on the credit side, all parades were cancelled. Each soldier had to carry in his pack and haversack everything he needed for the anticipated eight or nine days journey to Maymyo. A kit bag containing the rest of one's worldly possessions was loaded in Agra and would not be opened until the destination was reached. The journey to Calcutta, about eight hundred miles, took three days. Our troop train, as usual, having to give way to scheduled civilian passenger trains, which resulted in our staying for long periods in wayside sidings. As usual, we were packed six to a compartment. We pulled into a siding near Firozabad for the routine standard dinner of stew and a chapatti, followed by rice pudding and prunes, which had been prepared by cooks from the cantonment. Low caste beggar children, pot bellied and pitifully undernourished, and who invariably appeared to know of the arrival of a troop train, received a large proportion of the meal from the soldiers. They gladly accepted anything and everything; meat, potatoes, rice pudding and prunes, all went into one tin, proffered up with plaintive pleas and piteous eyes. There were also young girls, some carrying a half starved child on their hip, competing with the pot-bellied children for the remnants of the soldier's modest meal. These oft repeated scenes upset the most hardened soldier. Tea was brewed up late in the evening by our own cooks at another convenient siding near Cawnpore. A loaf of bread, a tin of margarine and a tin of jam were issued to each compartment of six men. Once again lots of beggar children bid for remnants of the meal. On the following days, prior to our arrival in Howrah and Calcutta, midday dinners were generally provided by cooks from the Cantonments that we were passing through - Gaya, Allahabad, Dhanbad etc. Most of the time travelling was spent playing cards with almost every compartment having its own card school game. Some groups were playing for money, some for cigarettes and some for matches - depending on the financial position of the players. A good standard pack of ten 'Players' cigarettes cost two and a half annas, a cheaper brand of 'Scissors' cigarettes, manufactured in India, cost two annas. It was a great feeling to get off the train and stretch one's legs, having been cooped up like chickens for the best part of four days in cramped and hot conditions; we were very dirty and sweaty. After a couple of hours spent on baggage fatigues, we moved over to the dock area, where the good ship 'Talamba' was moored.

The journey on the 'Talamba' from Calcutta to Rangoon took the best part of four days, a distance of about a thousand miles. The troops were so crowded that it would not be an exaggeration to say that you had to sleep standing up. I think the few officers on board, about twenty, occupied about one third of the accommodation available. The meals were a big improvement to those on the train being much more varied with well cooked fish at least once a day. It was quite often difficult to find a spot where it could be conveniently eaten. The Bay of Bengal was fortunately quite calm so there was little or no sea-sickness. On the whole, the journey was not too bad since we had very few fatigues, and to a great extent the troops were left to their own devises. Seawater showers were very, very popular, but the queues to use them were very long. However, everyone was very pleased when we docked in Rangoon and disembarked. I got my first glimpse of the world renowned, Shwedagon; the golden pagoda which proved to be a marvellous sight with the gold shining brilliantly in the sunlight and looking so calm and peaceful.

A troop train was waiting in the dock area on our arrival and when all the necessary unloading of the baggage from the 'Talamba' had been accomplished we set off on our rail journey for some 400 miles to Mandalay. 'B' Company was to go into Barracks in Mandalay for three months, while the remainder of the Battalion carried on for a further forty miles to the town of Maymyo. The train differed greatly from the Indian troop trains, it was more open, no three tiered bunks and all seats were made of solid wood and looked much more like a civilian train. The distances involved in Burma were much smaller than those in India, and the number of troops in India was vastly much greater; there being only two British Battalions in Burma - the Gloucesters, and the KOYLI. On leaving the dock area the train passed through part of the city giving the troops their first glimpse of Burma and its people. Initially it was difficult to differentiate between the men and the women because, except for the hairstyle, there was very little difference in dress. As the train stopped at various stations it was possible to observe the people a little more closely. Most were small in stature, very light browned skin, polite and almost shy. The women were extremely colourfully dressed, very clean and good looking with a full head of well groomed black shiny hair, mostly with a white flower, lotus I think in it. It was difficult to believe, as the medical officer had informed us at a mass lecture on the 'Talamba', that the great majority of women in Burma were infected with VD. He was of course, I think, grossly exaggerating with the intention of dissuading the troops from visiting brothels and shady night spots. He spoke of the deep sores in the thighs of unreported VD, the extremely painful treatment, a description of the instruments used in the treatment and the punishments metered out to those infected. Being only nineteen years old he frightened me and the others of my age.

The punishment for a soldier in the KOYLI who contracted VD was...

a) Reduction of pay to one shilling a day for the period spent in hospital; usually about six weeks.

b) After discharge from hospital, he was given ninety days defaulters (Confined to Barracks), with hardly a minute to spare from Reveille to Last Post at 22.00hrs.
c) He was not permitted to leave barracks for three months and not permitted to wear civilian clothes for three months
d) If four or more soldiers from one Company, about 120 men, were in hospital at the same time, that Company was confined to barracks until the number dropped below four.

These punishments were not in accordance with the Manual of Military Law, they were imposed by the Commanding Officer. I estimated that over 200 soldiers contracted VD during the four years spent in Burma, up to the mobilization in 1940. My platoon, which had thirty three Bandsmen, had eight cases of VD, one of which had been contracted at Kneller Hall, the Army School of Music, in the UK. He was returned to his unit in Burma where he was given the customary ninety days Confined to Barracks. In mitigation he said he had been infected by his girlfriend whom he had intended to marry, but she was, of course, a prostitute.

The journey, at about forty miles per hour was quite interesting and extremely varied. Initially we passed through many small villages with large duck ponds, paddy fields, banana plantations, inestimable numbers of pagodas with gold covered ornaments on the roof, and many laughing, smiling children. The countryside was much greener and the rail stations much cleaner than in India. I saw no beggars on the stations, or elsewhere, whenever the train stopped. In India, the great majority of women were veiled, only the eyes being visible. Here we saw no veils but pretty inquisitive faces. The monks (Phongyis) were however, reserved and unsmiling. At one of the stations we stopped at, Prome I think, the Commanding Officer purchased about 100 water melons from a vendor and issued them to the troops. They were cool and very refreshing, but made an awful mess in the train. We thought it very generous of the CO but found out later that he had reclaimed the cost from the PRI. The CO in question was Lt. Col. T.B. Butt, appointed to command the Battalion a few months prior to leaving Agra. I was surprised at the very large numbers on Phongyis (Monks), from small boy initiates to old men, in their saffron/ scarlet robes and severely shaved heads.

We arrived at Mandalay, the ancient Capital of Burma, after about twelve hours of steady travelling. On the whole, a fairly comfortable journey when compared with troop train journeys in India. We parted company with 'B' Company, who marched off to take up residence for three months in the barracks at Mandalay. The remainder of the Battalion vacated the present train and moved over to a smaller gauged hill train, which was to take us a further forty miles to Maymyo, a climb of over 3,500 feet. This train had an engine at the front and at the rear; one for pulling and one for pushing - which they took turns to do. It proceeded for about a mile or so before reversing onto a link line and climbing up the hill in the opposite direction. This manoeuvre was repeated many times before reaching Maymyo. The view of the landscape was truly magnificent. Jungle green covered hills, colourful 'flame of the forest' trees, tranquil and picturesque little villages, all with white and gold pagodas. The villages appeared to be well maintained and clean, the inhabitants well dressed and the dogs well fed. Bullock carts, much lighter than those in India moved at a leisurely pace, with the driver half asleep and smoking a cheroot.

The rail station at Maymyo was architecturally similar to those you would find in any small town in England. A small fatigue party was left at the station to unload the heavier baggage from the train and load it onto AT carts already lined up. The Battalion quickly formed up and moved off on its way to the barracks, about two miles distance, watched by a large crowd of European and local civilians. On the way we passed a Roman Catholic Convent and Church, a Church of England church with a large cemetery, an English restaurant, a Salvation Army establishment, two schools and a Tok H unit.

Bungalows, gardens and hedgerows were all well maintained and the grass, very green. It was as if we were marching through the English countryside. A carriage (Garry) stand stood immediately on the periphery of the barracks. The Barracks area was well laid out with lots of trees in a very green grassed area. The barrack huts, of one storey, were of wooden framed and large enough to accommodate about 40 to 50 men. It took a considerable time to clean and lock up one's rifle, draw bedding (three coir biscuits, pillow and two blankets) and find your kit bag from a dump of about eight hundred kit-bags which had been packed in Agra. There was no time to carry out a reconnaissance of the area, or of the town, before the 'Last Post' and 'Lights Out' were sounded.

For the next two days everyone was confined to Barracks and the next two days were fully taken up with fatigues of all kinds and getting the Battalion settled down in its new environment. Cleaning up the barrack rooms and surrounds was necessary, together with cleaning brasses and applying blanco to webbing. Rifles were inspected, and band instruments unpacked. It was about two miles to the town, which cost four annas by phaeton. The driver was keen to give his name and position in the Stand for our future custom. His name was 'Reggie' and I always hired him, whenever possible, for several years to come. The phaeton seated four persons quite comfortably, two facing the front and two facing the rear. His pony looked well groomed and well fed. He pointed out the places of interest with considerable pride, and after about ten minutes, moving at a nice steady trot, brought us to the centre of the town. Maymyo - may being the name of the British Officer who founded the town and Myo is Burmese for town.

In the town there were two up-to-date cinemas, both showing the very latest American and English films, a large Hotel/Cafe (the Unica), where I had many excellent suppers, two Chemists and two well stocked Wine Merchants. Port wine, which I now surreptitiously enjoyed, was one Rupee and four Annas a bottle for the best brand. There were also lots of confectionary shops, several gentlemen's tailors, a civilian hospital, two Banks and two large Departmental Stores; Rowe and Co and Jardine Matheson, a Post Office, Telegraph Office and a tall colourful Clock Tower. There were two well stocked Jewellers, a Japanese Photographer (K. Oda) and lots of teak furniture manufacturers.

In the camp area there were two football fields, one hockey and one rugby ground, an open air swimming pool, a six hundred yard rifle range and several married quarters. A large Military Hospital with well maintained gardens, a well stocked gymnasium, and an Officer's and Sergeants Mess. Each Company had its own Cookhouse and dining facilities. During the following months on route marches, training exercises and sports fixtures,

I realised how lucky the Battalion had been to be given such a wonderful posting. Throughout the year the climate was not too hot and not too cold. The town and its surrounding area would not have looked out of place in England. The botanical gardens and lakes were large and beautifully maintained and the Polo Club would have been acceptable anywhere in England. On the outskirts of town were lots of bungalows, with orchards and well maintained gardens, many of the occupants were of German, French and Italian origin. (The name bungalow is of Hindi origin - bangla meaning belonging to Bengal.) I knew of at least six Christian churches in and around the town. My favourite area was the large forest of eucalyptus trees, with the wide green fire breaks; perfect for running and keeping fit.

My brother James left Maymyo for England in December 1936, together with a considerable number of KOYLI who had completed their overseas tour or six years service. In late 1937, the Battalion left the cool, green and pleasant hills of Maymyo and moved down to Mingaladon, a small air station about twelve miles from Rangoon.

MINGALADON 1937

Hot, flat, and dusty, Mingaladon was a very big change from being in the cool green hills of Maymyo, which was in Upper Burma. Mingaladon is about twelve miles from Rangoon, its rail station about half a mile from the Barracks. The Barrack blocks were two storey brick with flush toilets, wash rooms with showers, but no baths. Within a few months of being stationed in Mingaladon, about one hundred soldiers were suffering from ringworm and crabs, (the latter being the name by which the soldier's identified the fungal skin infection 'tinea cruris'.). It was believed to be caused mainly by the poor quality of the laundry (dhobi) facilities, plus a few from VD. Mingaladon boasted in the way of entertainment, a small roller skating rink, a good football and hockey ground, a wet canteen (beer only), a supper bar, a gymnasium, rifle ranges and a good rail service to Rangoon. I spent lots of my leisure time on the skating rink and on the hockey ground. I played hockey for the Band team and also for the Battalion team. Whilst in Maymyo, I had also played for the Upper Burma combined team which consisted of Europeans, Indians and Burmans; Hockey was my chief love.

At Christmas 1937, except for the essential guards and pickets, we had three or four days free of all duties. We had the usual Christmas dinner of goose and a bottle of beer, served by the Warrant Officers and senior NCO's of HQ Company. Christmas day was one of the very few days when we did not have a chapatti for dinner. There were lavish portions of everything and everyone ate and drank to their full capacity, there being lots of surplus beer. The rest of the day was spent recovering or playing cards; gambling was more or less permitted as long as it did not cause any serious arguments. Fred Plowman and I went into Rangoon on Boxing Day by train. Fred was a close friend and fellow clarinet player. We had a very nice lunch at the International Hotel, the best in Rangoon, washed down by a bottle of the best port, at a cost of one rupee and eight annas. We roamed the town and local market for suitable presents for our families at home since we were both due for six months leave in March having served six years overseas. We bought a number of moonstones, opals, items of carved ivory, silk and a large number of cigars made from tobacco grown locally. My pay was 2s 9d per day, (due to rise to 3s per day on 23rd February, my 21st birthday), so I could easily afford these items as they were quite cheap, there being a thriving black market from the jewel mines in Upper Burma. Fred and I read a great deal and our tastes were very similar. Each time we visited Rangoon, which was generally once a fortnight, we each purchased a book; usually a Penguin paperback. We exchanged books after having read them and soon acquired quite a large collection. When members of the Band asked to borrow a book, we charged them one anna (1d), which we used to buy more books. Our library became so popular and profitable, that we extended to the Bugle and Signal platoons which brought in more money and enabled us to purchase a wider range of books including hardbacks and classical. When we mobilised on 23rd August 1941 in Maymyo, our range of books was much larger and superior to the official Battalion library. We never saw them again. Whilst waiting for the train at Rangoon railway station for our return to Mingaladon, I noticed a dental plate of three front teeth, which I recognised in a pile of vomit. Very few soldiers had dental plates; army regulations did not think them necessary except in cases where they were required to fulfil duties. I gingerly removed them from the smelling vomit and the following day I returned them to a very surprised and grateful Bandsman Ramsden. (He was killed near the Sittang river in 1942).

My brother Sidney left Mingaladon for the UK on the 29th December 1937, having completed his overseas tour of six years. He just had time to complete a sentence of seven days defaulters for being absent without leave at Reveille call on the 20th December. He had spent the night in Rangoon at night clubs and at the flat of one of the many local hostesses and was too drunk to get back to barracks before Reveille.

In the afternoon on the 4th March 1938, I departed from Mingaladon on the start of my journey to England for a long awaited six months leave. I expected to leave Rangoon on the 6th, take three days on the boat to Calcutta, a few days in Fort William in Calcutta, three days in the train across India to Bombay, leave Bombay on the 15th and expected to reach England by mid to late April. I was on top of the moon and much excited at returning to England. Two of my friends from the Band, Plowman and Reed, were also returning on six months leave with me, together with about twenty other soldiers from the Battalion who were returning to the UK having completed their six years tour of duty.

SIX MONTHS LEAVE MARCH 1938

Six months leave was the entitlement after having spent six years overseas. The alternative was to transfer to the home Battalion (1st KOYLI) with the possibility of that Battalion being posted overseas which would commit one to a further tour of six years overseas. By taking leave, I would stay with 2nd KOYLI who, it was rumoured, was due to return to the UK in 1941, a further two years only. The boat to Calcutta took three days which everyone thoroughly enjoyed. It was a civilian P&O boat and we travelled 2nd Class; no duties or fatigues, four to a cabin, clean sheets and pillows, good food and plenty of room on deck. No Reveille and a duty-free bar. We were rarely out of sight of land and we moved slowly and smoothly up the Arakan coast northwards. The Bay of Bengal was quite calm, with few passengers being seasick, everyone enjoying the freedom from military discipline and the general relaxed civilian atmosphere. There were many Indian civilians travelling 'Deck passage', which meant that they cooked, ate and slept on the open stern deck. They were very crowded and noisy, and the smell of curry mixed with the gentle sea breeze wafted from the many cooking pots up to the 2nd Class passengers. The toilet for the deck passengers was a small square canvas covered fixture overhanging the stern of the boat and was for use by both men and women. As we entered the mouth of the Ganges and the river Hooghly, we passed close to myriads of every type and shape of boat, all entering or leaving the very busy Port of Calcutta.

On arrival in Calcutta we made our own way to Fort William, a fort little changed since the mutiny, and but a few minutes walk from the centre of the city. After drawing a blanket from the QM Stores and selecting a 'charpoy' (roped bedstead), I went with my two friends to explore whatever the city had to offer. The main street, Chowringhee, was very crowded with every type of vehicle; clapped out old buses, rickshaws, bullock carts, ancient cars and trucks plus vendors of every description, stray mangy dogs, wandering bullocks and a mass of swirling humans. On one side of the road was the wide green Maidan, on which stood the Victoria Museum, a massive marble building with a large squat figure of the aged Empress at the entrance. We had not proceeded far down the street when we were accosted by a couple of supercilious Regimental Police who demanded to see our ET outfits; condom and tube of ointment. Fortunately we were all in possession of this equipment, which was standard with 2 KOYLI regulations whenever proceeding out of barracks. None of us had any intention of using them since we were on our way to England. I was still a virgin and it was common knowledge that Calcutta was rife with VD and many other medical ailments.

The punishment in 2 KOYLI for soldiers contracting VD was very, very severe. We came across masses of beggars pleading for buckshees - alms, spare cash or any unwanted item. It was believed that, many of them had been purposely crippled at birth to ensure they would provide a living for the rest of the family. There were several who had their legs grotesquely and permanently twisted around their necks rendering them totally incapable of movement, except for shuffling along with the aid of their hands.

The cinemas were very clean and fully air-conditioned - it was the first time I had ever been in an air conditioned cinema. I was very impressed and the contrast with the street and pavement outside was enormous. For eight annas I saw the film 'Three Smart Girls' starring Deana Durbin. We had a very good mixed grill and a bottle of beer at Firpos restaurant for the price of one rupee, before making our way back by foot to Fort William. As we had no late night pass, we had to be back in barracks by 9.45pm, and were informed that we were due to leave Calcutta the following afternoon, and so were unable to see more of the city. I was, however, billeted in Calcutta for several weeks in 1945, when I learned much more about this filthy, over-crowded city, endemic with cholera, smallpox and malaria, poverty stricken but an extremely busy and industrious city.

Early next morning, we moved by truck to Howrah rail station and boarded a troop train for Bombay, together with about two hundred other soldiers who had assembled in Calcutta. Two soldiers from the KOSB who should have been on this train, had been killed a few weeks previously by tribesmen on the North West Frontier, and had been brutally mutilated, their stomachs being ripped open and filled with stones. The station was extremely crowded with hundreds of Indians asleep on the platform wrapped in a single sheet, together with vendors of every description and lots of wandering mangy looking dogs. On civilian trains leaving the station there were more people hanging on to the outside of the train than inside.

The journey to Bombay took the best part of three days. It was hot and crowded and, as on all troop trains, slow and uncomfortable. We gave way to all civilian trains, which resulted in spending a considerable time in railway sidings. I did not mind as I was on my way to England after six long years overseas. I had left when I was just fifteen years old and five feet tall, and now I was returning at the age of twenty one and almost six feet tall, full of confidence and looking forward to a wonderful six months holiday.

The three days dragged by inexorably. The nights were the worst, with uncomfortable wooden bunks, smelly sweating bodies and swarms of mosquitoes with very little to see of the outside world. Whenever the train stopped, day or night, it was surrounded by hordes of beggars; thin naked pot bellied children and emaciated young girls suckling babies. They looked up to the soldiers with such genuine pleading eyes for the few scraps of food or buckshees that the soldiers could offer. It was sad to see humans in such a pitiful condition. As on nearly all troop trains, the water supply failed after the first day, so there was little opportunity to wash or shave. When we stopped for breakfast and a mug of tea, it was customary to save a little of the tea for a shave. A wash had to wait until we reached Bombay. The toilet, about two and a half feet square and six feet high, was basic and primitive with an indication on the floor where one should place one's feet and a hole in the floor that one had to aim at. There was no water to wash it away and it was obvious that there were lots of bad 'aimers'. It became quite smelly and required considerable dexterity when visiting. I was very pleased when we reached Bombay and boarded the troopship. We were allocated our mess deck, somewhere near the bottom of the ship. I thoroughly enjoyed a cold shower of sea water. My memory is fading but I think it was the 'Dunera', I have travelled on seven troopships and this is the only one whose name I am uncertain of.

We left Bombay on the 15th March, on the troopship (Dunera) calling in at Aden, Suez and Port Said, picking up troops from these stations, who had completed their overseas tour and were reverting to the home establishment or who were taking leave, similar to myself. Fred Plowman and I volunteered to attend and help out in the First Aid post; we had both passed our annual first aid courses. It entailed an hour's work in the morning, an hour in the afternoon and being on stand-by throughout the day. We were excused all other duties and fatigues. We passed very closely to a troopship in the Red Sea, proceeding eastwards. Showers of useless topees and shouts of rude sympathy from our ship echoed across the water to the east bound soldiers. I had experienced a similar meeting six years earlier, when I was on the ship going east. Later, in the Mediterranean, we passed an Italian troopship on its way to Abyssinia. Being excused all duties and fatigues, made life onboard enjoyable, almost like a holiday cruise. I was a little sorry for the soldiers detailed for potato peeling which went on all day; sufficient potatoes had to be peeled for over a thousand personnel.

Wallace Reed, the other Bandsman, volunteered to act as one of the two Mess orderlies for the whole of the three weeks journey. This was a duty that few soldiers wanted since it entailed drawing the food for the twenty or so soldiers on the mess table and washing up and cleaning the mess area after each meal. It was an arduous job going up and down stairs carrying the food from the ship's galley, especially when the sea was rough. There were many occasions when Mess orderlies, plus the food they were carrying, tumbled down the steps in an awful mess. Whatever could be salvaged, was cleaned up and eaten without any complaints as no-one relished the job of Mess Orderly. Whoever volunteered was given one day's pay (three shillings in my case), from each member of the Mess deck. Wallace was always 'broke, he liked to gamble at cards and invariably lost. Boat drill was carried out daily at 10.00am when everyone onboard paraded adjacent to their allocated lifeboat, wearing a cork life jacket. Initially it was interesting, preparing the life rafts and going through the drill of lowering the life boats, but doing the same thing day after day, became a little boring. The captain of the troopship, followed by a large retinue of subordinates, carried out a strict daily inspection after boat drill had been completed. The day to day monotony was broken by inter-unit boxing competitions, rifle shooting from the stern of the ship at a variety of targets thrown into the sea, games of hockey played with an expendable knot of rope, tug-of-war where you could not see the opposite team - they were on the opposite side of the ship and housy-housy (bingo). Gambling at cards and crown & anchor were strictly taboo, so if you did participate, it was necessary to have paid look-outs for the police.

Plowman and I took the opportunity to go on a voluntary route march when the ship docked for a few hours at Port Suez and again at Port Said. It was good to stretch one's legs on 'terra firma' and have another brief look around these two extremely crowded and busy Ports. From one of the persistent incessant vendors following the marching soldiers, offering lewd photographs, condoms, sweets, fruit and aphrodisiacs, I bought a packet of 'Spanish Fly'; the vendor said it was the real thing. It was suggested and agreed by the other members of the party, that we spike Wallace's drink and then carefully watch for some interesting developments. Wallace was of solid stature, six feet tall with a rough and humorous character. His face and neck had numerous warts, pock marks and many other blemishes of various colours. He was a person prone to accidents and misfortune. On one occasion he bragged that he had, over the plank (a night visit to a nearby Burmese village), and stayed with a sweet, clean young girl. For several weeks he tried to impress us with her beauty and his love life, his gifts to her and his successful escapades with the military police. Alas, it did not last for he contracted a large dose of VD and spent six weeks in hospital on one shilling a day. On discharge from hospital, he was given ninety days CB and a loss of all other privileges. On another occasion he "stood in" at a Company boxing competition for a colleague who had withdrawn on medical grounds; it was imperative for someone to fill the vacancy and so obtain at least one point for the Company. Wallace was knocked all around the ring for three rounds, barely striking a blow in return, but he was still standing at the end of the bout. His face was severely bruised and swollen and on blowing his nose, his left eye popped out of its socket which necessitated a few days in hospital. He drank his tea without any comment as to its taste. Although we maintained a close and vigilant watch on him, we were extremely disappointed to see no reaction whatsoever. We had been 'done' by the vendor.

JOURNEY BACK TO ENGLAND

I now looked forward to a pleasant, cool and smooth voyage of seven days through the Mediterranean and I was not disappointed as the weather was pleasantly warm, the sun shone all day and every day and the sea was very calm. I had no fatigue duties other than my couple of hours on the first aid post. I had plenty of good reading material and spent many hours watching the myriads of fish, of beautiful colour shape and size, swimming alongside the ship. The sharks were large, dark and sinister looking. I had seven very pleasant and leisurely days.

As we rounded Gibraltar and passed into the Atlantic, the weather suddenly changed, the sea became very rough and it rained and became much colder. From Bombay I had slept on the upper boat deck avoiding the smelly two decks below. From Gibraltar, and for the next three or four nights, it was too cold and wet to stay on the boat deck and so I was compelled to go below and brave the disgusting smell. This was my second passage through the Bay of Biscay, not as rough as the first time but rough enough to give me a permanent loathing for the Bay.

At last the day dawned when we sighted England - an enormous cheer from 1,500 throats. The majority of soldiers had left England for India at the age of eighteen years and were now returning at the age of twenty four years - a good reason for a hearty cheer. We docked in Southampton, adjacent to the Queen Mary, which made our troopship look quite small. Movement Control (Royal Engineers), who had come on board prior to the ship docking, issued the necessary documents and warrants for onward movement; mine was a rail warrant for York via London. Early next morning, everyone was impatiently waiting for the order to disembark. When it was finally given, 1,500 soldiers endeavoured to be the first ashore, taking no notice of the Customs Officials. They were perhaps accustomed to such behaviour and thought that soldiers on 3 shillings a day would have little to declare.

I enjoyed the comfortable journey to London, no hard seats, no flies and no beggars. The train travelled at a steady speed, allowing me to drink in views of the countryside. The train made several stops and it was interesting to see passengers getting on and off and listening to their conversations on current and local affairs. I was utterly and completely out of touch in this new mans world. The fields looked so small, but very colourful and the grass so green. It was an interesting and enjoyable short journey. The journey from London to York I found most disappointing, it was so quick because I was on the Mallard, a new and very fast train. I think the first stop was York, taking two hours. I wanted to see the stations we passed through, people getting on and off the train, their chatter, their news and views on current affairs, their accents and their dress. I was very disappointed. I did however enjoy the view of the countryside, but everything else was just a blur since the train was travelling about 120 mph. I recognised nothing, not even the stations until the train slowed down at Selby and I recognised the Abbey and a few minutes later my uncle William's house at Riccall. York station appeared very big to me and was very crowded. I was conscious of my ill fitting khaki uniform and my out-of-place topee. I had planned to take a tram from the station to Fulford, where I could get the bus to Kelfield. I was very surprised to see that the tram lines had been taken up - so no tram. I therefore took a taxi from the station direct to Kelfield. I was extremely surprised at the narrowness of the roads and the closeness of the hedgerows to the road; everything seemed to be in miniature. I sat with the driver and thoroughly enjoyed the ride.

Alice, my sister-in-law was alone in the house at Moor End, Kelfield when I arrived. She said, "Hello, we expected you three days ago, what was the hold up"? I did not point out to her that I had come half way around the world, on two ships and several different railways and that it was quite possible that I could have been three weeks late. She informed me that my brother Charles and brother Sidney had gone to the local, the Grey Horse, and would I like a cup of tea and that my board would be £1 a week. I agreed the board but declined the tea. It was about seven o'clock and the tea pot must have been on the hob for about three hours and quite stewed. I took a steady walk down to the 'Grey Horse', it was a pleasant evening and the air was fresh and cool. I saw that Kelfield had changed very little since I had left six years ago. The houses were the same, the gardens were the same, the ditch at the side of the road was the same and the cow pats on the road. The 'Grey Horse' had not changed, I noted that the urinal was still the wall against the back door. My brothers, together with about six other men, were seated on the same high backed wooden benches, playing dominoes. The room was extremely thick with smoke. I enjoyed my first pint of John Smiths on English soil for over six years.

Sidney, who was on his terminal leave, was also lodging with Alice and Charles, no doubt a welcome £2 a week. Charles was earning £1 13s a week as a farm worker - for a six day week. They had a family of three boys.

ENGLAND (APRIL) – NOVEMBER (1938)

I had only been in England about two months when I received a letter from the Infantry Record Office informing me that I should report to Southampton in July for return to 2nd KOYLI in Burma. No reason was given for cutting my leave down from my six months entitlement, to four months. I was extremely annoyed and replied that I considered it most unreasonable and that in the circumstances I wished to purchase my discharge. Anticipating that my request would be successful, I went to Leeds to ascertain if I could join the Leeds City police. Fred Plowman, who lived in Leeds, accompanied me. After several oral and written examinations, I was informed that I would be accepted if my discharge from the army was approved. I had no great wish to leave 2nd KOYLI but I was very bitter at my leave being reduced and no reason given. I had had only one small leave of seven days in 1935 during my tour of six years in the East.

The two bandsmen, Reed and Plowman, who had come on leave with me, left Southampton in late July. I would have been with them but for the fact that in early July, I had been informed by Infantry records Office, that I could purchase my discharge and that it would cost me, if I remember correctly,

£37. Alas, thinking that my application must have been turned down, I had spent the money which I had put aside for this purpose. I was now practically broke and did not want to borrow this considerable sum. It was only pique and bitterness that had initially made me apply for my discharge; I still liked and enjoyed army life. I waited until I considered the troopship had passed Gibraltar, three days, then informed the Record Office that as they had been so slow in replying to my application, I concluded that it was being refused and having spent the necessary money, now no longer wished to purchase my discharge. The majority of Regular soldiers at this time had a very low opinion of the Record Office and the War Office, considering them to be run by geriatric civil servants who had little real knowledge of the day-to-day running of the army. This view was confirmed later when I was posted to the war Office in 1956, where the majority of the staff, of the branch to which I was posted, were old and ignorant of the most simple and rudimentary facts of army life and organisation. There were no more troopships proceeding to the Far East until October, so I was able to take my full six months leave; and an additional six weeks! I left Southampton for Burma on the 11th November, on the oil fired troop ship? This second outward journey was very different from my first one in March 1932, when I was a very young and green Boy soldier. I was now one of the oldest 'sweats' on the ship and knew all the 'ropes'. I intended to enjoy this journey. Again, I was the only OR soldier from the KOYLI on board; I kept myself very much to myself, I was almost a stowaway and so avoided all duties and fatigues. It was a very pleasant, relaxing and enjoyable three weeks journey. I had plenty to eat and good books to read and in general the sea was quite calm and the weather perfect. We stopped at Port Said for supplies and then moved on non-stop to Bombay.

Bombay was quite cool - a pleasant 60-80*F. I obtained, with a little difficulty (one old soldier to another), a second class ticket to Calcutta. I should have travelled on the troop train. I used this ticket to visit Agra and Lahore in northern India. I wanted to see whether I could locate the tall Afghan who became more like a friend than a Canteen Wallah, in the four years that I was in Agra. I spent several days in these military stations, having my meals in the local hotels. I stayed in the 2nd Class Waiting Rooms, at the railway station, at night. I eventually made my way to Calcutta, where after spending a day or two looking around the city, I reported to the military in Fort William. I was informed that 2nd KOYLI had moved from Mingaladon to Maymyo and was given a ticket for the journey to Rangoon by P&O steamer.

This second journey to Rangoon from Calcutta was very much different to the one

I made on the 'Talamba' in March 1936. I had a cabin to myself, nice clean sheets and pillows, plenty of good food and the bar was open all day. I was surprised by the large number of German civilians onboard, friendly and very inquisitive. It was a very pleasant and comfortable three/four day's journey. I spent two days in Rangoon having my meals in the Imperial hotel and the nights in the station waiting room. I visited the two main night clubs, Maxim's and Apex, both appeared very dowdy and decrepit. The hostesses were all well past their prime - unless you had spent at least one year in the jungle. These two clubs are where my brother Sidney came to drink and where my brother David came to dance.

I travelled by civilian train to Mandalay where a Company of KOYLI were stationed. I had to change trains here to the smaller hill climbing train, which twisted, reversed and huffed and puffed its way around the hills for forty miles to Maymyo. I arrived in Maymyo on the 23rd December having been away from the Battalion for nine months. I was broke, the carriage fare from the railway station to barracks had taken my last eight annas. My brother David was extremely surprised to see me as the two Bandsmen that had returned to Burma in August had informed him that I was purchasing my discharge. He had sold (flogged) all my kit, boots, shirts, jackets, slacks, vests and polished leather equipment - everything. I was not only broke but had absolutely no kit whatsoever. What a homecoming! Fortunately it was possible to obtain everything I needed on credit and I had well over six weeks pay due to me. I had bought a large quantity of chocolate and cigarettes with me from England, so there was considerable interest in my luggage - kit bag. Unfortunately, I had also placed camphor balls in my kit bag, with the result that both chocolate and cigarettes were heavily impregnated with camphor. In addition, they had suffered six weeks of rough handling and hot conditions. No one complained and nothing was thrown away. My brother David and I were the only two of the Price family now serving in the regular army. My brother James had completed his engagement on 11th December 1936 and Sidney, on the 21st June 1938 and Albert on the 10th December 1938. All three of them, still on the Regular Army Reserve, were recalled to the colours in August 1939 prior to the outbreak of the Second World War.

From now on it was back to army life in Maymyo. It only took me a day or two to re-kit myself, make myself at home and readjust to army life. I was a little rusty on the clarinet but after a week or two, this was quickly rectified. I enjoyed my hockey, playing generally three times a week. If I wasn't due to play for the Band, Company or Battalion, I walked over to the hockey field and made up any team that was a man short. If there was no shortage, I went for a run by myself, in the eucalyptus rides (fire breaks).

I played football for the Band and also for HQ Company. I played rugby for the Band - I was not interested in cricket. I enjoyed long distance running, especially cross country running for which the country around Maymyo was most suitable. Life in Maymyo was very good and a long way from the European war, although the war in the West did not really start in earnest until May 1940. Many of us felt a little guilty at being so far from the action - after all, most of the Battalion were Regular soldiers. However, we didn't know it, but our turn was soon to come. In the meantime, we took advantage of the present peaceful situation. I went to the cinema twice a week, a ticket cost eight annas, and saw the very latest American and English films. I had lavish suppers at the 'Unica' twice a week, generally a mixed grill - a full plate of all known meats, washed down with a glass of the best Port wine, followed by a comfortable open carriage ride back to barracks. I was in the Dance Band, playing the clarinet and saxophone, so had many evening engagements. It was at one of these dances that I met Sheleagh, my future wife. We were able to meet generally twice a week when we would go to the cinema or for long walks to the Botanical Gardens and Lakes, or into the eucalyptus forests - green, peaceful and quiet. On many occasions I sneaked back into Barracks, avoiding the Military police, a short time before Reveille. I remember whilst on field training at Kangi

Camp, in the Shan States about thirty three miles from Maymyo, I walked back to Maymyo on the Saturday, returning to Kangi very late on Sunday, just to meet Shelagh for one night.

We married on the 10th February 1941 in St George's Church. We had one hundred guests which included the Band, with instruments. The reception was held in the Masonic Hall. The cake was made by an Italian restaurateur by the name of Angelo, assisted by a Greek called Christie. Years later, in 1945 in Calcutta, I met both of these men when I went into a cafe for supper. In addition to the cake, they also made one hundred separate pieces of cake, each piece being wrapped in rice paper and embroidered 'F' and 'S' in silk. We had a hogshead of Scottish McEwens beer. The total cost of the wedding was 100 Rupees (less than £8). We rented quite a large house on Avenue Road, for less than 30 rupees a month and there were no other rates or taxes.

On the 1st August every year a full Battalion parade was held to commemorate the Battle of Minden, which took place in Germany on 1st August 1759. After various drill movements had taken place, including the march past, the parade formed three sides of a square. Following these movements, the Colonel, sitting on his horse (he rarely got off it) informed the Battalion in a very loud voice of the gory details of the Battle of Minden and the heroic part played by the KOYLI. Many of those on parade had heard the speech several times and could recite it word for word as good as the Colonel himself. On completion of the parade the rest of the day was a holiday - the best part of the commemoration. White fabric roses were worn on topees on this day. In the evening the Officers held a Ball the other ranks (OR's) held a Dance - OR's could not hold a Ball. The dance was held in the gymnasium and I was present in the Dance Band. Everything was going very well, the drunks behaving reasonably well, when news reached the gymnasium of a soldier being killed in the Unica Cafe in town. It was much exaggerated and blamed on the local Burmans. My brother Sidney was in the Cafe at the time and said that it was partly an accident. The soldier, intoxicated was leaning back in his chair when one of his friends from 'A' Company gave him a push causing him to fall backwards. He hit his head heavily on the stone floor and died almost immediately. The dead man's friends, in a drunken state, quietly left the gymnasium and armed themselves with bayonets, having the intention of avenging their colleague. This could have developed into a very serious incident but for the quick thinking of the RSM, who halved the price of beer at the bar and turned out soldiers from another Company, who blocked all the exits from the Barracks. There was a Court of Enquiry, but it never caused any discipline problems outside the Battalion.

Early in 1941 signs of war were looming in the Far East. Local papers carried vivid pictures of dreadful atrocities being committed by Japanese troops in China. Bayonet practice was performed on live Chinese prisoners, sword practice in beheading by Japanese officers and much worse. Nanking, which had been well illustrated in 1937/8, was still fresh in one's memory. The Free French authorities had granted permission for Japanese troops to move into Indo-China. War was coming. The Battalion set itself the task of improving its fitness and efficiency in preparation for the worst. Every member of the Battalion had to be proficient with rifle, Bren-gun, grenade, signalling by Morse code and semaphore, compass marching at night and general efficiency in the jungle. On another occasion we had an endurance march which had to be completed without stopping during the whole of the thirty miles. It was a warm day and it took place in the hills around Maymyo; we carried full kit. Although a full water bottle was carried, discipline rules did not allow you to drink from it. But on this occasion, the majority of bottles were empty long before returning to barracks. I saw some of the men drinking from unclean streams. About one hundred of the men (20%) dropped out through exhaustion and had to make their own way back to barracks under their own steam. I remember this particular march very well, for it was the toughest that I had ever done. On completing it and arriving back in barracks I had to walk up three or four steps to the Barrack room. My legs would just not change the rhythm of level walking. It took a great effort and time to drag myself up those few steps. After dumping my equipment and locking my rifle in the rifle-rack, I jumped on my bicycle, with considerable difficulty, and rode to my married accommodation. I drank a pint of cold milk, two pints of cold beer, had a cold shower and was violently sick afterwards, but was feeling much better.

On another occasion, I took part in a Platoon night compass march when there was no moon. We were given several compass bearings where we had to report to an umpire to prove correct completion. Several of the bearings took us through thick lantarna country. Lantarna is something like a gooseberry bush but many times larger and its scratch is fairly poisonous. We crossed a fairly wide and deep stream at least three times our compass bearings having been deviously arranged, so as to take us repeatedly through this stream. The mule carrying ammunition panniers got stuck in the mud several times and it was with considerable effort and much cursing that we managed to free it. It was morning, the sun just appearing over the horizon, when we arrived back in barracks, tired, wet and very dirty. After a short cycle ride to my married accommodation, I got out of my wet and filthy clothing and thoroughly enjoyed a cold shower. My body was almost completely covered in scratches from the lantarna. Sheleagh painted every scratch with white iodine.

There were quite a number of deaths in the Battalion whilst stationed in Maymyo, I believe about ten of which two were suicides because of the shame of contracting VD, one blowing his brains out on the rifle range and the other by standing in front of a railway train. Two drowned in a lake whilst on training. A Boy soldier by the name of Crisp died from a bamboo scratch on his leg. Gangrene set in and his leg had to be amputated, but sadly he died. Another died from rough play by his friends in a cafe. All were buried in the military cemetery, about half a mile from the barracks. Being in the Band at the time, I attended most of the funerals. It was a large cemetery with tombstones of soldiers from the many regiments that had been stationed in Maymyo since the early 19th century.

On the whole, Sheleagh and I had a very pleasant but hectic six months of married life; dances, cinema, enjoyable walks in the Rides (fire breaks) in the forests. I played lots of hockey and football. Jungle training, field and weapon training became very severe at times. We were all Regular soldiers and realised this was necessary and could soon be put to the test. There were few complaints. It was at this time that I was promoted to full Corporal. In early August it was fairly certain that the Battalion would soon be put on a war footing and considered to be on active service. Misdemeanours would then be considered in a different light, absent without leave would become desertion, striking an NCO, disobeying an order, damaging one's weapon etc would be very grave offences. All civilian clothing and private possessions had to be packed up and stored in the gymnasium, uniform to be worn at all times. I had to sleep in Barracks.

THE BATTALION GOES TO WAR

The Battalion mobilised on 23rd August 1941 and moved to 'Taunggyi' (Taungdwingyi) in the eastern Shan States. I was posted to 'D' Company as Sergeant of 16 Platoon. Here we carried out extensive jungle training in very thick bamboo, tall elephant grass and jungle covered hills. It was here that we all discarded our topees and were issued with the Bush hat, which was already worn by the Gurkhas. We also dumped the Lewis gun, long overdue as it was an old gun and subject to lots of stoppages because of bad design and manufacture. Each Platoon was issued with a Bren gun, which was a very accurate gun and free from stoppages. We had ample .303 calibre ammunition for them and soon became proficient in their use. On one occasion I personally fired hundreds of continuous rounds from it to see whether I could find a malfunction. The barrel became so hot I thought it was about to melt and droop while the pile of empty cases was burning my elbows, but still no malfunction. A few months later when conditions were not so good, the gun got very dirty and the working parts had to be greased with fat from tinned sausages - it still never malfunctioned; a good and accurate gun which the soldiers used with complete confidence. 'D' Company was also issued with one .5 Anti-tank rifle, a useless and cumbersome weapon in the jungle. I fired three or four rounds from it and discovered that it had a nasty kick back which bruised the shoulder. Later when the Battalion was in action, it was carried for many, many miles without ever being fired in anger. It was accidentally dropped in a river when the Battalion was in retreat.

The Battalion stayed in the Taunggyi area for almost three months. We were accommodated in bamboo Bashers, which were constructed entirely from bamboo. Each Basher accommodated about forty men and was about sixty feet long and twenty feet wide, a gangway about four feet wide extended centrally the full length of the hut which was open at both ends. Each side of the gangway was a bamboo platform, about two feet high for sleeping and storing equipment, rifle and bedding. The roof was covered with banana leaves, which made it fairly waterproof. The camp was about two miles from the town, which had little to offer the troops in the way of entertainment or food. There was a wet Canteen and a Supper bar, run by a civilian contractor by the name of Wazir Ali, where it was possible to purchase beer, eggs and chips and egg and bacon sandwiches. Food supplied by the Battalion cooks generally consisted of meat rissoles for breakfast, stews of every variety for dinner and jam and bread for tea; plentiful and never declined.

Field training was extensive and hard, the troops had very little or no free time and bed time was generally welcomed. I remember on one occasion when we had to cross a river, which was about 150 yards wide but looked much wider, my Platoon was detailed as point and to cross over in full kit, rifle, pack and haversack, and hold the opposite bank until the remainder of the Company came over using rope lines. On entering the water it was impossible to immediately get down into a swimming position, my water-logged boots kept me in an upright position. After a few minutes however, I managed to adjust my body and swim successfully across to the far side, dash up the bank, lay down absolutely knackered and fire off a few blanks - with water from my pack running down my neck into my face. The rope line broke on two occasions and several non-swimmers were in real danger of drowning. Experienced swimmers, who were completely naked, had been positioned on each bank of the river in case of this happening, but it was a miracle that no-one was drowned.

A few days after the river crossing, 'D' Company camped near to a large pond/lake, after a very long and exhaustive march. One of the soldiers quickly stripped off and jumped into the water. Immediately he was covered from head to toe in black leeches and jumped out of the water much quicker than when he jumped in. He was surrounded by laughing smokers who touched the leeches with the tips of their cigarettes causing them to immediately fall off. It took about thirty minutes to remove them all.

Periodically I was detailed to carry out the duty of Battalion Orderly Sergeant. One of the duties was to see that the Wet Canteen was closed and all soldiers were back in their Bashers by 10.00 pm and all lights out by 10.15pm. I went to the Wet canteen a few minutes prior to closing time and noticed two soldiers, Martin and Ansell who were always the last to leave, were not present. Martin had been a Boy soldier with me for at least three years and I knew him very well. I checked their Basher but both were missing. Returning to the canteen, which was run by a civilian contractor, I discovered that one barrel of beer was missing. I knew that if I could find the barrel I would find M and A. I guessed that they would have gone down-hill from the canteen with the heavy barrel and soon found them about one hundred yards away, happy as two larks and unconcerned at their folly, but very intoxicated. I made them carry the barrel, which they did with much difficulty, back up the hill to the canteen and settle up with the contractor (Wazir Ali) to his satisfaction - they were his best customers. I informed Martin that if they both went immediately to their Basher without any noise or trouble I would not put them under arrest. A few weeks later, I heard CSM Housley say that Martin and Ansell were the most troublesome pair in the Battalion in peace-time, but two of the best soldiers in war conditions.

On 1st December 1941, the Battalion moved further north-east to Loilam and a week or two later, to the Salween River, several miles east of the town of Takaw. It was at this location that the KOYLI were to dig extensive defence positions in anticipation of a Japanese attack coming from the rail-head at Chiang Mai in Siam. The Salween forms the border between Burma and Siam and in this area runs between mountain peaks, some 7,000 ft high, and is one of the fastest running rivers in the world. The jungle is dense on both its eastern and western banks and the sun only shines for a short period at mid-day. For the next seven weeks the KOYLI dug extensive and elaborate trenches, built barbed wire entanglements and fences, and machine gun fire lanes on the western side of the river. Alas, all in vain for the Japanese, having full control of the 'Bay of Bengal' moved mainly unopposed, into Burma from the south.

We left the Salween gorge in late January and boarded a train somewhere near Kalaw for Moulmein/Martaban in the south. About two hundred of our men were infected with malaria during our stay in the Gorge, which made the Battalion seriously under-strength, yet we had not fired a single shot in anger. At Hainale, a small rail station still on our way south, the CO was ordered to proceed to Thaton, a large town a few miles north of our original destination. The situation had changed and the position had become more serious. We arrived at Thaton on the 2nd February and were bombed by Japanese planes two days later; our first taste of the real thing. In extreme panic the whole of the civilian population fled the town leaving everything behind, pets, personal possessions, prepared meals on tables, and shops and stores fully stocked. We tried out our Bren guns (LMGs - Light Machine Guns) using the heavy cumbersome high tripod on the fast moving planes. It was absolutely useless, we never got anywhere near a hit. On all future attacks by aircraft we used the Bren gun as a rifle, it being quicker onto the target and both easier and much more effective. We dug our slit trenches much deeper and with much more vigour than in the past. We suffered only one casualty; he had fallen into a well while trying to take cover. I endeavoured to revive him and I thought I was being successful and he was showing slight signs of recovery when the Battalion FAP (Forward Aid Post) took over. He had been in action against the Germans in Norway while serving with the 1st Battalion KOYLI in 1940. We saw our first wounded soldiers, Jats, Dogras and Gurkhas, who were being evacuated through Thaton. After two or three days in Thaton, A Company was ordered to proceed to Martaban where they came into contact with the enemy. There was much confusion regarding orders and loss of mules and equipment. A Company arrived back in Thaton a few days later both tired and hungry. One man had been wounded and two were lost in the jungle or the dark. My Platoon carried out a patrol some ten miles south east of Thaton where we had information of a Japanes presence. After producing a little ineffective rifle fire against some doubtful targets, we moved on after making no real contact. On or about the 12th February, we moved to the Bilin river area. I did several night patrols over to the east bank of the Bilin and on each occasion I selected the men I considered to be the most suitable for such patrols. Privates Hunter, Gomersol, Hutchinson and Caddick were four of the men I remember well. We were permitted to choose the weapons we wished to take - rifle or Tommy gun. On each patrol I also carried two grenades, some soldiers preferring not to carry them, and we muffled our boots with socks. Prior to going on one such patrol my brother David, a Motor Cycle despatch rider, turned up a few minutes before I was due to move off with a letter from Sheleagh written in December. I crept under a blanket and using matches and cigarettes, managed with great difficulty to read it. The nights were very dark and we were on unfamiliar ground. We had no knowledge what-so-ever of the whereabouts of our own troops Indian or Gurkha. Surprise contact with them in the dark could be more dangerous than meeting the Japanese and proved to be quite tricky. The Japanese were to be expected anywhere and everywhere. It was also very dangerous when returning to one's own area with several patrols suffering casualties from trigger happy sentries. On one occasion the sentry was killed when the patrol mistakenly returned fire. I saw no useful purpose or reason for night patrols for we gathered no useful information, and probably did more harm than good.

On 16th February, my D Company was detailed to move into the village of Danyingon on the west bank of the Bilin and about a mile or so from our current position. It was a nice day and we were not expecting any problems. We understood that the village had been checked by the Company Command the previous day so we were quite relaxed. My Platoon was leisurely leading the way into the village when, coming up to the centre of the village we were extremely surprised to see about twenty Japanese happily enjoying bathing at a well. They were naked except for their loin cloths and completely unarmed. We were very surprised, and so were they, but we recovered the quicker. I was in the leading section of the Platoon and was six or seven yards from my first eye-ball to eye-ball with the Japanese enemy. They started to run for some huts and some vegetation on the left of the road where they had presumably left their arms. I shouted 'Stop' to the nearest one to me, a stupid thing to do, but of course he did not stop, and I fired from the hip but missed. I then took careful aim and shot him between the shoulders. He fell flat on his stomach. I rushed up to him and found him to be quite a pale-skinned Japanese. I looked down at him and, as I prepared to put another bullet into him, I wondered what it would be like too stick my bayonet into this soft white meat, but it was not necessary as he was quite dead. No blood was coming out of the hole in his back so I must have hit his heart. This initial action must have taken less than ten seconds. The rest of the Platoon was picking off the bathers and I got one more. Two or three of the bathers did manage to reach the huts and take cover in shrubbery. The platoon, without hesitation or orders, gave chase after them. The first hut that we came up to had some six or seven noisy disorganised Japanese on the open ground floor, the enclosed second floor was on stilts. I gave the order to the men nearest to me to fire three rounds rapid fire into them. Why three? - We were automatically taught to count the number of rounds we fired. This ensured that your magazine was never unexpectedly empty. I considered that three rounds would be sufficient. A volley of about thirty rounds, a few screams and groans and no Japanese left standing; we considered them all to be dead. On hearing the outbreak of firing our 17 and 18 Platoons must have taken cover and must have been concerned as to what action they should take since there had been no time for us to communicate with them. Rifle fire was now coming at us from both the right and the rear. A few yards from the next house we came up to I spotted Jack Hirst the senior Sergeant in the Platoon, lying trapped under the

Platoon's dead mule. The animal had bolted on the sound of firing and had dragged him off the road and into the bushes, where the Japanese had shot it and also thought that they had killed Jack. He feigned death and was a very lucky man. The Japanese close to him fled into the bushes on our approach. We moved wearily on in the same direction we had taken when chasing the bathers, passing through several maintained gardens with fruit trees and pineapple vegetation. Very wearily we checked several houses as we moved forward, but no Japanese. Moving along a narrow pathway a tallish Japanese Officer, smartly dressed with nasty looking eyes and raised sword, rushed out of the bushes at me. My bayonet was on my rifle and I could have easily reached him, being only about three feet away, but I instinctively put a bullet into his chest at point blank range. The bullet appeared to lift him off his feet within one second, and whilst he was still upright I put another bullet into his chest. Japanese now appeared to be everywhere and bullets were coming from all directions, those coming through the pineapple vegetation made a peculiar hissing sound. When a soldier standing very close to me was hit in the chest, he gave a long deep sigh and fell. We had certainly walked into a veritable hornets nest. Having commenced the action as hunters, we were now the hunted. Eventually we came out at the west side of the village where we took up a defensive position in a shallow decline about one hundred yards from the village.

Although we still got the occasional bullet coming our way, we were not disturbed by the Japanese. They must have been too busy reorganising themselves. I had now experienced my first very close contact with the Japanese and felt surprisingly quite calm. The rest of the Platoon was calm, alert, but unusually very quiet. Except for the casualties we had suffered it could have been just another day on the Assault course. We had been trained for such a day and reacted automatically. We had killed a considerable number of Japanese, but we had also lost some friends. Later in the day we were joined by 17 and 18 Platoons. The Company was now about thirty to forty strong and the Company Commander, Captain Wardleworth, decided that we should put in an immediate attack on the village. We carried out the attack a little north of where 16 Platoon had emerged from the village, in open order and at the double for about 150 yards. The attack was fairly successful, but we did lose two men. One man, slightly in front of me, was hit and dropped without a sound. We did not stop, orders forbade it. We managed to get about fifty yards into the village where we were engaged and became fairly static, in fact, bogged down. We had been given no firm orders as to what action to take once we were in the village. Should we push straight ahead regardless or should we spread out left and right - it was a large village and we were small in number. The Company Commander had not deemed it necessary to question members of 16 Platoon as to their experience in the village and, after about two hours of taking pot shots at the Japanese, we were ordered to withdraw, which we did in some disorder. We had achieved very little and we had lost some more men. It had been a very long day, we had not eaten since early morning and we were very tired. The next morning, several stragglers from A Company arrived in our area, one of them being my step-father Jack Rowley who told me that A Company had been taken completely by surprise early in the morning by an overwhelming number of Japanese. Casualties had been extremely heavy, including my brother-in-law, L/Cpl McDonald, and the unarmed CSM Bill Housley. A Company had been positioned a little over a mile south of our position and we knew nothing of B and C Companies except that they were also somewhere on the west bank of the river.

The following day, a full Battalion of Gurkhas, probably four to five hundred strong, attacked the village with great vigour and determination. The Japanese replied with heavy fire and shouts of opposition. I got a close and clear view of the action in which probably up to a thousand men were engaged in hand-to-hand close combat. The noise of gunfire and the screams of the combatants were awful, as close to hell as one could get. Just prior to entering the village a Gurkha was hit in the backside. He pulled down his shorts, checked the bleeding wound, pulled up his shorts, grinned at me and dashed into the village. The attack went on for several hours, but it failed to take the village. The Gurkha casualties must have been extremely heavy. I couldn't help thinking how lucky 16 Platoon had been in getting out of that village without suffering more serious casualties than we did. The date of this action was probably the 21st, (or possibly the 17th or 18th) but this is just a guess since we never knew the date and we never knew what day it was; all we knew was that the sun came up and the sun went down.

On the first day of our retreat we covered about fifteen to twenty miles. The tracks we moved on were thick with dust and we were occasionally bothered by the odd Japanese plane and marauding Japanese patrol, but we suffered no casualties. We stayed the night in Kyaito where a large number of our troops were concentrated in a camp. We had a good hot meal and a quiet night's rest and early next morning we began our march to our next defensive position, the River Sittang. During the night B Company had joined us, having made a very difficult cross-country march from its northern position on the river Bilin, it too had suffered considerable casualties. We were bombed and machine-gunned by both British and Japanese planes and initially we thought the Japanese were using British planes captured in Singapore and had not bothered to change the markings - what else could we think? On one occasion, still under air attack, we were moving through open ground, a rubber plantation with small young rubber trees well spaced out in regular lines, I took cover in a small dip in a track way about twelve inches deep - no real cover but the best available. A vast number of machine-gun bullets were ploughing up the earth and were coming directly towards me. I braced myself for the impact, but they stopped about five yards from me. A very, very close shave! My lucky 'Blue Eyes', on my bush-hat was still holding. Empty shells, point 5 inch calibre and British made, fell all around. One soldier with a touch of 'Deolali' walked aimlessly about heedless of the shouts to 'get down'. Fortunately, he had a charmed life and was not hit. The British pilots were cursed more than the Japanese pilots. After this had gone on for some considerable time, we felt justified in returning fire to both Japanese and British. We suffered a few casualties, but far fewer than expected - we were very lucky.

As we neared Mokpalin and the Sittang river my Platoon, which was leading, saw considerable movement in some trees and bushes parallel to the river. We moved forward cautiously in open order not knowing whether they were friend or foe because we had no binoculars. Much to our relief they were Gurkhas, but we realised that this could have been a serious accidental engagement. My D Company took up a position 200-300 yards from the Sittang river and to the south and west of Mokpalin about 800 yards from the Sittang bridge. Late in the afternoon a patrol of about twelve Japanese were seen coming across the paddy field towards our position, directly toward my Platoon. We waited patiently for them to get closer, anticipating a good kill. When they were about 250 yards away, still not close enough, some idiot from another Platoon some distance on our left, opened ineffective machine-gun fire which permitted them to disperse and get away. We were very angry and cursed the premature firer. He had spoilt an easy kill which would have raised our spirits, and generated a few plus points to offset our hurried and uncomfortable withdrawal from Danyingan. On the whole, except for a few bursts of rifle fire, the odd mortar bomb and shell, we spent a fairly quiet night. I can't remember when we had last eaten, but everyone was very hungry and drinking water was scarce. I slept fairly well, boots on, no bedding - we had not had any for several weeks. A pack for a pillow, my rifle at my side, morale was high, discipline was good and we were confident in ourselves and for the future.

A shattering and extremely heavy explosion at about 4.00 am woke everyone that had managed to sleep. The echo of the explosion reverberated round the hills for several seconds followed by a long stunned deadly silence. It was immediately obvious that the bridge over the river Sittang had been blown. It took only a few minutes for everyone to grasp the situation, especially the non-swimmers. It was unbelievable that it could have been blown by enemy action. Up to a thousand troops had marched up to and crossed the bridge and a great number of troops, Gurkhas, Indian, Burmese and British with all their weapons, vehicles and equipment were within a few hundred yards of the bridge and were waiting to cross. There were also all the troops we had left at Kyaito a day or so earlier to consider. The decision to destroy the bridge was taken by Major General John Smyth.

(Part of the original text written by Major Price is missing from this point.)

Communications between the various groups that were heading for the Sittang River Bridge were tenuous to say the least and, for some, had been completely non-existent over the last two or three weeks. There appeared to be no other explanation than, it had been blown by our own command. The Japanese did liven up with rifle fire, but they were not between us and the river or between us and the bridge in any real strength.

Lt Colonel Keegan, our Commanding Officer, walked slowly from Company to Company chatting to the men and showing no signs of fear of the sporadic rifle fire from the Japanese. His cool manner and attitude certainly gave everyone's confidence a lift up but, unfortunately, Colonel Keegan was seriously wounded in mid-afternoon. My Company 'D' stayed in position until late afternoon when Japanese planes were still active. One very brave but careless pilot came over our position very low at tree top height machine-gunning us. Everyone fired at him, using every weapon to hand, a veritable hail of bullets hit him and he crashed about 150 yards from our position. A very large number of very angry troops, Gurkhas and British, dashed over to vent their anger and sufferings of the last few days on the pilot. He was, however, already very dead.

Sporadic fighting continued until about 5.00 or 6.00 pm when a general disorganised and undisciplined dash to the river took place. My 16 Platoon managed to keep together as far as the river, after which the situation became quite chaotic. Sergeant Hurst, and several members of the Platoon, took the bamboo roof from a hut and got it to the river. So many men jumped on it, which caused it to sink and it was lost in the current. We had to try something else. Hundreds of troops were now milling around on the edge of the river, confused and undecided as to what they should do since there were no boats and no rafts. The river looked very wide - a rough guess about 700 yards, so it was swim or be taken prisoner. The despairing and hopeless look on the faces of non-swimmers was awful. I had never swam this far and doubted whether I could manage it; it did look very wide.

I took the bolt and magazine from my rifle (No 425, which I had owned for six years), the detonators from my two grenades and threw the lot as far as I could, into the river. I discarded all my clothing, shirt, shorts, socks, boots, hat and my AB 64 with a photograph of my mother, which my uncle William had sent me. I was still wearing my wrist watch, which I had forgotten and my dog-tags around my neck but I was now naked. I picked up a piece of bamboo, about five feet long, put it under my left arm and indicated to members of the Platoon how it was possible to cross to the west bank. Sergeant Hurst and many others of the Platoon did likewise, even though some of them were worse swimmers than I was. I jumped into the river and with considerable trepidation started to paddle and swim to the west bank. Japanese planes were still active. I cannot remember how long it took me to reach the west bank, but it was a long, long time. The current, which was not very strong, carried us diagonally across the river so we probably swam and paddled about 1,000 yards. The water was fairly warm and buoyant and Caddick, a Platoon member, was the first of our group to reach the west bank, giving a loud yell of delight when his feet touched solid ground. It gave those of us, still struggling along encouragement to keep going. The Platoon was now split up and scattered. Some did not make it, some landed several hundred yards further up the river. There were those who had not attempted it and those who decided to try their luck further up the river north of the bridge. Unfortunately, a large number of the Battalion were taken prisoner.

So we made it, exhausted but elated. We took a long, long rest to recover from our fatigue and to await the possible arrival of other members of the Battalion. Over the next two hours or so exhausted and wounded swimmers, many with flesh, arm and leg wounds, staggered up the west bank all fiercely cursing the blowers of the bridge. A few with chest and abdominal wounds had managed to cross on the odd raft and small boat. The majority were naked or half naked and the west bank was completely deserted, except for those arriving from the east bank. There were no signs of any defensive positions having been prepared, or the fully armed Brigade that had crossed over a day or so earlier. My number 16 platoon was now down to about eight men, unarmed, bare footed and mostly naked. Sergeant Hurst and myself, who had both been in Burma for five years and had a good knowledge of the layout of the country, decided that we should strike north until we hit the railway then follow it west; the men who had only been in Burma a few months readily agreed. From the people in a small Burmese village nearby we borrowed some bits of clothing to cover our naked 'bits and pieces'; they also offered us some cold boiled rice and water. I had always found the majority of the Burmese people very friendly, but on this occasion I think they were very pleased to see us on our way. They must have heard the sound of battle on the east bank of the river and didn't wish to become involved.

We hit the railway about a mile west of the bridge, but there was still no sign of the phantom Brigade or of any west bank military. We moved painfully and slowly, for not one of us had boots, for about two hours. It may have been some four miles when we noticed a large deserted baggage dump about a hundred yards north of the railway. Tearing open the bales of sacking, we found large stocks of boots, socks, KD shorts, slacks and shirts, webbing equipment and enormous amounts of 'Queens' Christmas puddings. We ravenously filled our stomachs with the rich fruity Christmas pudding until we could scarcely breathe since we had no drinking water. We then kitted ourselves out with perfectly fitting uniforms, boots and web equipment. Hurst found a .38 revolver and I found a .32 pistol with a few rounds of ammunition. We filled our packs with puddings and commenced our journey westwards, well dressed, well fed, thirsty, and with restored confidence. After moving westward for about two hours we heard the sound of a train coming up behind us. As it came closer, we heard the sound of drunken singing with a broad Yorkshire accent. We made ourselves known and the train, consisting of three or four flats, stopped and made room for us. There were about thirty or forty naked and half-naked men on board, my brother David being one of them. We were very glad and relieved to see each other. Also on board were several cases of whisky and rum. We were very thirsty and they were very hungry. I can't remember the exchange rate between whisky and puddings but everyone was satisfied.

The driver of the train, a soldier with some knowledge of railway engines who had managed to assemble the flats and engine a mile or so from the bridge, suggested that we, being so well dressed, thought we were f.....g officers. The train stopped at Pegu, some thirty miles from the bridge where the remnants of 16 Platoon disembarked expecting that this would be where stragglers would initially report and where reorganisation and re-arming would take place. The train continued on its way to Mandalay with the wounded plus a few other men who had decided it would be better to continue to Mandalay, possibly a hundred miles north and where a KOYLI detachment was stationed. David stayed on the train and reported in at Maymyo, where his wife Dorothy was expecting their second child, Allen, who was born on the 24th February. Still half naked, David visited Sheleagh who, on the 24th kitted him out with some of my clothing which she had in our married accommodation. She also arranged for him to have a bath and a meal prior to him going to the hospital to see his newly born son.

Five or six officers and possible more than 200 KOYLI stragglers reached Pegu. After the sick and wounded were evacuated, there were less than a hundred fit men, demoralised and very angry at the blunder and debacle at the Sittang Bridge. There were no arms, clothing or equipment available and no mess eating utensils; you were given a handful of boiled potatoes or rice into your hands. After a few days things somewhat improved and rifles, ammunition, grenades, Mess-tins and some eating utensils appeared. Clothing, which I did not need, and some spades for digging slit-trenches were also issued, but there was still much confusion and disorganisation. The KOYLI was amalgamated with the Duke of Wellington's Regiment forming two Companies. A number of incidents that occurred at this time remained in my mind for many years afterwards. I well remember having to dig a slit trench in a leper cemetery, disturbing many skeletons and having two or three sleepless nights because of the eerie atmosphere. One day a soldier threw a grenade into the Pagoda fish pond to obtain some fresh fish. Zeroing my rifle a short distance from the camp, caused considerable consternation and a few jangled nerves. Some joker placed a set of web equipment and a bush-hat on the Pagoda Buddha. I think we stayed about six days in Pegu and thankfully saw no sign of the Japanese.

Early in March, we marched to the village of Hlegu, about thirty miles south west of Pegu where there was a vital river crossing. On this occasion, General Wavell visited the unit and informed the CO that the unit should endeavour to, "Live off the country". Assuming that there was some hidden meaning behind the General's comment, that night Hurst and I checked his transport for food etc, but all we found were lots of full petrol cans. Hlegu is about twenty miles from Mingaladon where I was stationed in 1937/8. Amalgamation with the Duke of Wellington's Regiment [DWR] ended with Colonel Tynte remaining in command of the KOYLI. We had no idea what we were supposed to be doing, and no signs of any Japanese. We had barely settled down when we were on the move again, this time by trucks to Tharrawaddy, about seventy miles north.

We were more confused when, within hours of arrival at Tharrawaddy, my Company (by this time reduced to about Platoon strength) was ordered to go back the way we had come to a place called Hmawbi, about thirty miles south, where it was reported there was a Japanese road block. Colonel Tynte set out with 2nd Lt. G.C. Cranfield and his platoon in a truck to do a reconnaissance of the block. Unfortunately, the Colonel was shot in the stomach by a Japanese sniper and died. The Platoon (now of about section strength) continued under 2nd Lt. Cranfield and proceeded to within half a mile of the block. We stayed the night in a small clearing about thirty yards from the road. There was lots of rifle and mortar fire from the block and from south of the block. We were unable to ascertain the Japanese strength in the block, or the strength of the forces south of it, but by the amount of fire directed on the block it was considered to be very strong. About 10.00 or 11.00 pm, the noise of firing died down to the occasional odd rifle and mortar round. A short time before midnight, we heard the sound of marching feet. 2nd Lt Cranfied sent Corporal Howson, who spoke both Urdu and Burmese, up to the side of the road to try to identify who these men were. The noise they made was unbelievably loud and must have been heard by the forces, south of the block. Howson was not absolutely certain who they were; they could have been Indian, Gurkha or Japanese. He reported to the Lieutenant who then accompanied him to try to make a positive identification of these men. After about an hour Cranfield and Howson returned and reported that they were convinced the men were Japanese. The marchers continued to pass for about an hour and, although we were only a dozen or so men, we did have grenades and plenty of ammunition. We could have killed a great number of the marchers before disappearing into the darkness. We were not absolutely certain who they were; they could have been friendly forces but, if they were Japanese, what were they doing coming from the direction of the road block? What a decision to be taken by a very junior Lieutenant! The Lieutenant decided to stay put, stay quiet until the coming of daylight then, jump in the truck and move north as fast as we could, our dash to be covered by the tank. Just before dawn the plan was yet again changed. We would sneak out on foot, leaving the truck and the tank to follow as soon as we were away. This was carried out successfully without any casualties or contact with the Japanese. I later learned that the marchers were Japanese and they were the main Japanese force that occupied Rangoon. What a close shave! We joined up with a unit (Company/P1) a mile or so north.

Next day we continued moving along the railway, marching in single file on both sides of the line which was on a raised embankment. A close friend and drinking pal, by the name of Taylor (Nutty), was leading at point with his section when a machine-gun, manned by Japanese and Burmese, opened up. Everyone was taken by surprise, especially Taylor who was very close to them. The Japanese were also taken by surprise and had only manned the gun seconds prior to Taylor getting within fifty yards of them. Men quickly took cover by rolling down the embankment and returning fire. We suffered about ten men killed, one of whom was my father-in-law, Jack Rowley. It could have been many, many more. I and about six other men took cover in a small clearing surrounded by bushes and from our position we could clearly see a fairly well built tall red-painted house with windows adjacent to the railway and close to the spot where the machine-gun had opened fire. I saw men dressed in Burmese clothing running toward the house. I fired at one of them and was about to fire again when a Captain, newly arrived from Maymyo, stopped me and said not to fire on Burmese. A few minutes later, a shot from the vicinity of the house killed a 2nd Lieutenant standing close by; he had only been with us a day or two and we did not even know his name. The Captain was mute and we blasted the house, the windows and anything that moved. We did not go and occupy the house and the 2nd Lieutenant was very dead; he looked very, very young and at peace. I later learned that his name was Ableson - he is mentioned in the book 'No Maymyo - No Mandalay' and is listed in Corporal John Heald's Roll. Taylor, my friend, the nearest man to the machine-gun, did not even receive a scratch. The dead were left to the scavengers, human and animal. An army retreating and disorganised, and after Sittang demoralised, is not a pretty thing. We continued our journey north hot, tired, thirsty and hungry. We had been informed that we were to move north to Yenangyaung for rest, re-equipping and reorganisation. I have a very vague recollection of how far, and for how long, we marched before reaching Yenangyaung, but it was not, "partly by train and partly by steamer", as quoted in the 'History of the KOYLI', but a long, hot, foot slog. It was Officers and a chosen few who did it the easy way.

I remember passing through Magwe because it was there that I met Lupe Lane, an ex Boy soldier and Bugler, who had recently arrived in Magwe from Maymyo. He told me that Sheleagh, my wife, and my son Michael had been in Magwe a few days earlier and had been evacuated by air to India. I was greatly relieved to know they were both safely out of Burma. I had not heard from them for several months and was very disappointed that I had missed them by only a few days. The RAF had already vacated Magwe and moved north. I saw an abandoned fighter, which appeared to be in good condition, which suggested that the RAF had left in a great hurry. We continued our long slog north and reached Yenangyaung, the large oil fields in central Burma, on 17th March, tired, footsore, scruffy and dirty.

Lt Colonel Chadwick, who had been in hospital with malaria, took command of the depleted Battalion. About 100 KOYLI from the detachment in Maymyo, and some from the hospital, joined the Battalion in Yenangyaung. Together with these recently joined men I think the strength of the Battalion was still barely 200 men. The oil fields, except for a few engineers, had been abandoned. We settled ourselves down in the abandoned but well built bungalows with real beds, and in some cases with sheets, refrigerators and swimming pools. Food was reasonable, the best we had tasted for weeks, and there was a bar in the town with a limited variety of drinks. I took off my boots for the first time for weeks and washed my shirt and shorts, in which I had sweated profusely both day and night for several weeks. I swam in the clean water pool and slept in a comfortable bed without fear of being disturbed by the Japanese. Life was very good having such marvellous comforts.

Many of the Officers managed to arrange trips to the comforts of Maymyo, allegedly for dental treatment and other doubtful aches and pains. Sergeants Hirst and Scott, great friends of mine, who had girlfriends in Maymyo told me they were planning to spend two or three days there, or some miles to the north. They asked if I would delay reporting them absent for as long as possible saying they would definitely be back within three days. Unfortunately, the Battalion moved back south before they returned and both were declared as deserters, a very serious offence. Hirst joined Calverts force in Maymyo and was later taken prisoner by the Japanese and died of wounds in Mandalay jail, while Scott, on the return of the KOYLI to India, served a jail sentence for desertion.

A makeshift reorganisation of the Battalion was made whilst in Yenangyaung. Platoons were called Companies and Sections Platoons. Bullshit appeared in the shape of drill parades. A CSM told me that I was not shouting loud enough when giving drill commands. I was annoyed and showed it. I had been taken off showing my new Platoon the danger and benefits of the grenade. How to prime it, throw it, ensure that the pin was in a position for quick throwing, timing the throw after pulling the pin and taking the best position after throwing; also that one grenade, at least, should always be carried. Many of the men had never thrown a grenade. I considered it much more important to get to know the men, where they came from, how long they had been in Burma and what were their experiences etc, rather than 'Sloping and Presenting arms'. The order to drill was stupid and showed a lack of commitment and responsibility when the time could have been spent on real preparation for what we knew was to follow.

The Battalion was fully equipped with boots, rifles, bayonets, unlimited amounts of ammunition, grenades and two or three mortars, which were never put to full use. My platoon filled their web pouches with thirty to forty rounds of ammunition. Several of the men agreed to carry at least one grenade, but some were a little apprehensive of carrying them; I always carried two whenever possible. In the bungalow in which I was accommodated I found a creditable map of the Irrawaddy and its tributaries. I kept it, thinking that one day it could come in handy. I noticed that there were motor boats of all shapes and sizes on the river close by and that fuel would not be a problem.

We left Yenangyaung in the early morning of 11th April in 3-ton trucks. Crowded and sweaty we travelled south for about fifty miles and arrived at a fairly large Headquarters late at night. Next morning we moved a few more miles to a large road junction which, I think, was Thitagauk, where we spent a quiet and peaceful night, but could hear distant gunfire and heavy explosions. No sign of any Japanese, but double sentries were put out as a precaution. Early next morning a large convoy of 3-ton trucks carrying Gurkha troops, passed through our position and proceeding north. They appeared to have been in recent action with the Japanese as they had a considerable number of wounded. At this point we began to feel a little isolated and vulnerable. By mid-morning a small squadron of tanks appeared and gave us a lift to another road junction, a few miles to the north- west, where a cart track led to the village of Toksan, some eight miles away and where the tanks turned around and headed back north. It was a hot and dusty two hour march to Toksan. As usual, we did not know where we were going, or why, or what to expect, other than the Japanese. The rank and file were never, 'put in the picture' so there was little wonder lots of 'cock-ups' and chaos occurred whenever we became split up, as we often did. Quite possibly the CO did not know himself. Communications between units and formations were bad to non-existent. Since the Sittang tragedy there had been so many changes, so many reorganisations, so much renumbering of Companies, Platoons etc, plus the fact that we were subject to so many attachments and reattachments to Brigades, Headquarters and Formations, it was little wonder we were often confused, lost and felt we were every-ones dogsbody.

It was late afternoon when the Battalion, in reality two small Companies the size of Platoons, reached a small track junction about 150 yards north of the village of Toksan. I was given two men and told to check whether there were any Japanese in the village. The two men must have had similar thoughts and feelings as I had. Basically, we would be walking targets and we would know the answer a few seconds after being shot. There were still a considerable number of Burmese residents, men, women and children, lolling around. They were quiet and looked apprehensive, not aggressive, but certainly not the usual smiling faces. We walked right through the village, looked into two or three houses and back again, rifles at the ready and fingers on triggers. I also had a grenade with the pin straightened for quick throwing. We felt very, very vulnerable and our backs very wide. If there had been any Japanese in the village we would have been 'dead men'. My luck was holding, there were no Japanese in the village. I was told to wait at the junction with my two men and direct a Company of KOYLI, about twenty-five men, with transport carrying the Battalion's mortars, Vickers machine-guns and QM stores due in a few hours in the direction that the Battalion had taken. I was not informed of the distance the Battalion was going - they probably did not know themselves. The Battalion moved off on its way in the late afternoon or early evening leaving the two men and myself at the junction. There was still no sign of any Japanese, only the odd reconnaissance plane. As darkness fell I took the two men, one had a touch of malaria and the other had the 'craps' (a persistent need to go to the toilet) about 150 yards west of the junction where some trees and bushes alongside a sunken east/west track provided some cover from attack from the south. It was a cool, dark, starlit and peaceful night. I kept watch while the men slept.

Late at night, or in the early morning, a patrol of about fifteen to twenty men coming from the west passed within inches of our position and proceeded into the village. I was absolutely positive that they were Japanese from their talking, and they were not concerned about the noise they were making. As they entered the village, they kicked a barking dog - the yelp of pain from the dog was very distinctive. I woke up the two men and told them of the position and that we would take no action at present. An hour or so later, the sky was lit up by the lights of several lorries approaching the junction. They lit up the whole area and must have been seen for miles around: the Japanese patrol must have been licking its lips. I made myself known to the senior Officer - Captain Miller (ex RSM). I informed him of the direction of the track which the Battalion had taken, but that I did not know the distance that they had intended to travel. I also informed him of the patrol, and that

I was positive they were Japanese. His exact words to me were, "Don't give me the shits Price". He said that he intended to stay the night and join the Battalion in the morning. I thought it a stupid and irresponsible decision and suggested that he should move on but, if he was determined to stay, he should put out double sentries. I informed him that my duty was now completed and that I would take my two men, for whom I was responsible, to my original position about 150 yards to the west. I was determined not to stay with him and his lorries. Captain Miller had several lorries in his party and about twenty five men. The lorries appeared to be well laden but were not positioned in any sort of defensive way. I cannot recollect there being any AT carts in the party, as stated in the 'Regimental History' or in the book 'No Mandalay - No Maymyo'. (The latter is a complete fairy tale as far as Toksan is concerned.) The AT carts could have arrived an hour later. Mules travel at about four miles per hour, whereas lorries travelling slowly will cover at least twelve miles per hour. The road they had travelled on was very good and the track they had travelled on quite reasonable. I had travelled on the road and had walked the track just a few hours previously. I was up and about long before daylight. I did not have long to wait for what I knew was going to happen; it was so obvious. Just before daylight, the Japanese patrol attacked making lots of noise, rifle fire, crackers which sounded like rifle fire, the odd grenade and a light machine-gun. The two men and I had a very clear view of the attack being only 150 yards away. They said, "What shall we do Sarge", I said, "Nothing at present". I could have given enfilade fire, which would have surprised the Japanese and probably made them withdraw, but I knew there were very few of them. I wanted to see what action Captain Miller was taking; he had been warned. I wanted him to have the 'shits'; his remarks to me still rankled and I was angry. The engagement lasted less than ten minutes. The whole of Miller's unit fled north, leaving all the lorries in Japanese hands. They had been taken completely by surprise and gave practically no opposition. I doubted whether any sentries had been positioned. We waited a few minutes, fired a few rounds at the Japanese on the lorries with the possibility of having hitting one or two of them. We then headed north quite leisurely, to where the rest of the Battalion were camped about a mile away.

Colonel Chadwick, the CO, quickly arranged an immediate attack to retake the lorries. A party of about twenty men, commanded by a green 2nd Lieutenant, recently arrived from England, was quickly formed. I was the only NCO in the party. We were to attack from the west and for some unbelievable reason were ordered to carry a number of spades. I asked the Lieutenant, "Why the spades?" he said that he had been so ordered. I told the men to lose them before we got anywhere near the lorries. Only an idiot would carry a spade when 'hand to hand' close fighting was expected. I was positive that they would not be required. We approached the lorries from the position where I had spent the previous night. Surprisingly, a considerable amount of rifle fire came our way, but initially no-one was hit. As we got nearer to the lorries the rifle fire became very heavy; two or three of our party were hit. We returned rapid fire on the enemy around and amongst the lorries. There were some minutes of deathly silence with no firing, then we saw a lorry coming toward us - we thought it was a Jap escaping with one of the lorries. We concentrated rapid fire on it, which brought it to an abrupt halt and was very surprised to see Captain Bootland (KOYLI) drop out of the driver's side severely wounded in the neck and throat. We had shot our own man. I was not aware that the CO had arranged for another party to attack from the east. I did not know whether the 2nd Lieutenant was aware of this, but if he did he certainly did not inform me, his second in command, or any of the men. We had fired on each other, which explained the heavy rifle fire we had encountered. This was another 'cock-up', with the men not being, 'put in the picture'. Some Japanese were killed but the remainder fled and were not seen again. The re-taken lorries were severely damaged, mostly by our own fire. We suffered three severely wounded; Captain Bootland the worst, and six or seven men with minor wounds. I suffered some small metal splinters in my legs and wrist, but the two in my legs were deep and to the bone. They caused me no real trouble, nor did they affect my mobility as both attacking parties made their way back to the Battalion carrying some of the salvaged stores from the lorries. I didn't have the pleasure of meeting Captain Miller at Battalion HQ. There were no other troops, British, Indian or Japanese in the immediate vicinity as is stated in the two books previously mentioned. A doctor was at the Battalion HQ and gave every injured man a tetanus injection. Bootland and two others, one an ex-Bugler, required special attention, morphine and special bandaging. The doctor had very limited medical equipment but someone made a rough type of litter using two bamboo poles and a ground sheet, hitched it to a mule and placed the severely wounded Captain on it. The mule moved forward about twenty yards then bolted, tipping the Captain out onto the hard ground; he was having a terrible time and looked very pale and sick. An AT cart was belatedly found and Captain Bootland and three other wounded men, who were also unable to walk, were placed in the cart. An AT cart is a fully metalled two wheeled vehicle drawn by mules, stubborn animals but very strong. Six or seven walking men joined the AT cart and I was put in charge and told to head roughly north-west until I hit the river Irrawaddy, which was several miles away, then turn north until

I met friendly forces. I had no map or binoculars and the sun was high in the sky. Our weapons for defence were four or five rifles, with doubtful users. Although I had a rifle, grenade and plenty of ammunition, we were still a very vulnerable party.

Initially I followed the rough track for about three miles. The solid wheels of the cart, plus the rough and uneven track, caused the wounded to be tossed and rolled about. They moaned and groaned incessantly, but there was little I could do to improve their condition. I periodically rested the whole party and gave the wounded a drink, except for the Captain for whom it would have been dangerous. I wetted his lips, wiped and cooled his face. I adjusted some of the bandages of the wounded, gave them a few words of comfort and reassurance regarding our position. I became more than a little worried when I spotted an empty bullock cart about two hundred yards ahead of us, blocking the track. I halted the party and went forward with two of the least wounded men to investigate. It appeared to be a typical Japanese road block with ideal covering fire from both flanks. We approached carefully from the east using whatever cover we could find as we went all the way around it. No Japanese, what a relief! We rejoined the AT cart and continued our journey. I am not sure how far we travelled, or for how long, but it must have seemed like an eternity for the wounded on the cart. Captain Bootland looked like a dying man. At one point it was necessary to leave the track to maintain the desired direction and travel over open country. The sun was still fairly high in the sky and the track twisted and turned - was I going in the right direction I asked myself? I assured the men that I was for I could not lose their confidence in me. I can't recollect how many hours we travelled, or how many times we stopped to rest the wounded to give them a drink and check their bandages. I had passed several First Aid exams whilst in the Band, but this was the real thing. Water was becoming a worry and some of the walking wounded were beginning to slow down. My legs were aching and painful and blood sucking flies were a nuisance. Late in the afternoon, or early evening (we had no watches) I spotted a Bren -gun Carrier about six hundred yards away. I knew that it was British because the Japanese had no such vehicles at this time. We made ourselves known and it quickly joined us. It was commanded by Captain J.T. A. Wilson (KOYLI), whom I knew quite well. He took Captain Bootland and the seriously wounded into the Carrier, saying that he would take them to the Brigade F.A.P. I was relieved to hand them over still alive for it had been a terrible journey for them. He directed me to where I would find Brigade HQ, a mile or so further north, which I found quite easily. After I had handed over the walking wounded to the Brigade F.A.P., I considered my responsibility completed.

I realised that I had been extremely lucky in not encountering roving Japanese patrols. I located a cook-house and had a large enjoyable meal of stew and a large mug of tea after which, I borrowed a blanket, the first I had seen or used for several weeks, found a nice quiet spot and had a very good undisturbed night's sleep. Next morning I had a good breakfast of bully beef, bread and tea. I visited the F.A.P. and was informed that the walking wounded were being moved north by trucks and that Captain Bootland and the severely wounded had already been sent to a hospital paddle-steamer on the Irrawaddy. I found myself amongst a motley group of Brigade staff, wounded awaiting evacuation and others like myself who had been separated from their units, and some who had just got lost after active engagements with the enemy. There was a great deal of confusion and movement.

On 15th April I and several other soldiers joined a composite Infantry unit commanded by a Lieutenant who had been ordered to take up a defensive position near a chuang, some distance to the north. (A chuang is a river, dry in summer and wet in winter.) After about an hour's march we arrived at the chuang, which was mostly dry but in some places about a foot deep. We moved to the north bank and dug a few holes, which couldn't be called trenches, and set up rifle and Light Machine-gun positions. Later that night, or early next morning, a great crescendo of machine-gun and rifle fire opened up on our left. It sounded like a major Japanese attack. We stood tense and alert and after about ten minutes it suddenly stopped. As daylight appeared, we realised that it was another 'cock-up'. Indian troops on the north bank of the chuang had heard movements on the south bank, assumed it was the Japanese and opened up with Light Machine Gun and rifle fire. British troops had arrived at the south bank late, and unexpected, but the Indian troops had not been 'put in the picture'. I later learned that it was a KOYLI unit that had been fired upon. We stayed in position another night, a very noisy night with lots of Light Machine Gun and rifle fire, but no close quarter targets. No sleep, a number of wounded, but I saw no dead in our sector. About mid-day on the following day we withdrew to Magwe, about ten miles north which was my second visit to this town.

I was not very keen on this Defence Platoon organisation that I had joined and asked the Lieutenant if he knew where the KOYLI were located as I would like to return to them as early as possible. I was certain that they must be very close-by. Unfortunately, I got no satisfaction. Although the Lieutenant kept in close touch with the Platoon, he probably had another appointment with the HQ. One aspect of being with the Brigade HQ was that I got a fairly good and regular meal. We only stayed in Magwe a couple of hours for a short rest then continued northwards. After about two hours march we came up to a fairly large chuang which was crossed without any major difficulties. The Platoon stayed on the north bank in a defensive position and the Head Quarters moved a few hundred yards further north. A quiet uneventful night for us, but some miles over to the east we heard the sounds of continuous heavy gun-fire. Early next morning we were shocked when we realised that the HQ had moved off without warning us. We guessed they had continued north, so we too headed north, hoping to catch up with them within an hour or two. For about the next two hours we moved north very quickly, covering nine or ten miles, but no sign of the HQ. After a rest, which we needed, we decided to continue moving north keeping the Irrawaddy on our left until we reached Yenangyaung, which we guessed not to be very far away. After a few more miles of marching we saw smoke over Yenangyaung. As we got to the outskirts of the town we saw signs of recent conflict, bodies of dead soldiers with dog-tags still on, abandoned equipment and rifles suggested a retreat in a great hurry. After a considerable hesitation we entered the town from the north east. The oil-wells were still on fire, belching out thick black clouds of smelly smoke, even the sky was blackened with the smoke. There were still a large number of British troops in the sector where we had entered the town, but no signs of the HQ;

they must have by-passed the town. The first two days were quiet and we were well supplied with tins of bully beef and drinking water. On our second day I, with a group of men waiting for orders, were very surprised when a QARANC (Queen Alexandra's Royal Army Nursing Corps) nurse in uniform walked unhurried passed us. She was wearing a belt and a pistol strapped to her waist. We all knew that the pistol was to ensure that she would never be taken alive by the Japanese. We felt very ashamed that our thoughts had been for ourselves when, only a dozen yards from where she had walked passed us was an overturned tank with the body of a soldier trapped halfway out of the turret. The next two days were nasty. The Japanese had entered the south of the town and contact was fierce and confused. It went on day and night and we got very little rest. We suffered quite a number of casualties both killed and wounded but the dead were left where they fell. The wounded were very distressed by the absence of medics. Orders were eventually received to the effect that every man should make his own way out of the town as quickly as he could. Not an unusual order since I had been given it several times in the past. The majority of the men in our sector had considered the quickest and safest way out was by river. I did also, knowing the area slightly from my previous visit to Yenangyaung. I was very surprised to see such a large gathering of troops on the river bank and realised there was little chance of obtaining a boat. I decided, and several other men agreed, that it would be better to follow the river northwards with the hope of finding a boat or meeting up with other retreating forces. We were getting tired and discouraged and it was getting dark when we came up to a large village where a Paddle Steamer was moored on the river. A wonderful and most welcome sight, but it was a FAP (Red Cross). Although none of our party was seriously wounded, we did have minor wounds, fever and exhaustion. We were given a good meal and a hot drink and a space to sleep; there were about ten of us. The open flat top deck of the steamer was filled with wounded, amputees and open wounds full of maggots and flies were everywhere. I spotted Captain Bootland sitting with his back to the rail, he looked much better than when I had handed him over to Captain Wilson a few days ago, but he still looked very pale and sick. I said that I was very glad to see him safe and in medical hands. He asked me to give him a drink from his water-bottle as he couldn't manage it himself; he had a rubber funnel attached to his mouth. I said that I was very sorry for giving him such an awful time whilst on the AT cart and wished him a quick evacuation to India. I never met him again. Early next morning a Jap fighter plane came straight toward the steamer with machine-guns blazing. We were sitting ducks on a crowded flat topped metal deck, with no-cover whatsoever. It made a second run with guns blazing but, to everyone's amazement he was machine-gunning a small armed patrol boat laid alongside the steamer. We realised how lucky we had been and that at least there was one civilized Jap in Burma. Our small party left the steamer, it being a Red Cross vessel and we were carrying arms. Our presence would endanger the lives of the wounded. The Japanese infantry needed no excuse to butcher the wounded.

We were given a good meal prior to leaving the Steamer, so we had a full belly and a full water bottle to start us on our journey. Our group consisted of stragglers from the KOYLI, the Gloucesters and the Duke's. We were well armed with rifles and plenty of ammunition and not encumbered with heavy kit, our dress being shorts, shirt and bush hats. I was the only NCO (Sgt) in the party. I told them I was heading for Mandalay, some 120 miles away. I told them that I had been in Burma for six years and knew the country well and had been stationed in Mandalay on several occasions. It would be safer if we stayed together as a fighting force, but it was for them to decide. I had no military authority to say what they should do. We stayed together. Japanese planes who freely roamed the sky, gave us no trouble. On our second day we had a slight skirmish at rifle range with a Japanese reconnaissance patrol, which showed little aggression and we were pleased to continue our journey. It was hot and dusty with food and water becoming a problem and our speed of progress limited to that of the weakest and sickest. I had been hoping to cover about twenty five miles a day, but this was perhaps too optimistic. Initially we had avoided going into the villages for security reasons as we did not know how close the Japanese were behind us, but we now needed food and water. The first village we entered was quite large with well built houses and well dressed inhabitants. They were friendly, but not the usual laughing smiling people I knew them to be. They were tense, worried and afraid. I spoke and gestured with the Headman since I could speak only a little Burmese. I told him that we were short of food and water and that we had nothing too give in payment. They willingly gave us cooked, boiled rice, fruit and filled our water bottles, with hints of smiles. They were pleased to see us leave and I understood why. This was repeated twice more before we reached our destination.

After five days and nights of very uncomfortable marching many of the men were close to severe exhaustion. Eventually we reached the bank of the river near Ava, five or six miles from Mandalay. The bridge had obviously been blown by the British. Except for a number of soldiers, about thirty in number who were wandering aimlessly about, the area was deserted. Signs of a camp, recently abandoned, were everywhere and we found some tins of bully beef and biscuits and had a good substantial meal, the best since leaving the Steamer. After a most welcomed rest, I walked along the bank of the river for about 1,500 yards, a short reconnaissance. I came across a group of six officers busily engrossed in map-reading and a few yards away from a camp fire where five or six chickens were being roasted in a large metal frying pan. I walked casually between the officers and the fire and as I passed the frying pan, I quickly nicked a fat, hot chicken. I put it under my loose shirt, carried on walking without breaking step and safely away. I would have liked to have seen their faces when they found that one of their chickens had flown the nest. I did think of going back to the officers and congratulating the cook, but thought the better of it. The C-in-C of course had said that we should live off the land, so perhaps I should have risked it. The officers, whom I presumed to be Staff Officers, moved off early next morning without a word of advice, suggestion, or recommendations to the soldiers lolling about. They should at least have told us of the latest up-to-date position. My already low opinion of officers dropped even lower.

A good night's sleep, a satisfactory breakfast of bully beef and biscuits and I was ready for anything the day had to offer. Although we had no idea of the present military situation, it was obvious that we should continue our journey to Mandalay as quickly as possible. Everyone, about thirty in number, agreed. On our journey from Yenangyuang to Ava, we had heard every day and night, heavy gunfire coming from the east where the north-south rail and roads terminated in Mandalay, so we had to be extra vigilant. We avoided the town where there was the sound of considerable rifle fire and headed for the very visible Mandalay hill and the Barrack area, which we reached without encountering any problems. We were completely surprised and disappointed to find the Barrack area deserted of all organised military authority, except for about thirty soldiers wandering aimlessly about. We had merely joined another bunch of stragglers! An hour or so before we had arrived, a soldier had shot a pig, using a Tommy-gun, an amateur butcher had cut it up, an amateur cook had roasted it and we had roast pork for supper. The total number of stragglers was now about fifty, consisting of Sergeants and below and from different Regiments.

The next morning we had a serious and sombre meeting. Every man had the opportunity to air his views and ideas on the situation we were in. We were all stragglers and, like me, for many different reasons and through no fault of their own. Some of them had been in Burma for a year or so, others for only a few weeks, but everyone realised the situation was extremely serious and dangerous. Some suggested going back west, over the Irrawaddy and Chinwin towards India, while others were for going further north over the two rivers and towards Assam. A third option was to go east towards Maymyo and the Eastern Shan States and the fourth option was to stay in Mandalay and be taken prisoners of war. All agreed that it would be safer to travel in groups, however small. I decided to continue going north and explained that there was less chance of meeting Japanese in large numbers at this early stage, and the rivers in the north would be easier to cross. We would be in Shan territory - the Shans had always got on well with the British and there was an airfield at Myitkyina (about 300 miles) east of Assam. About fifteen men, in the same condition as myself, joined me. Each man had a rifle, thirty or forty rounds of ammunition, some tins of bully beef, biscuits and a water bottle. There were lots of beef and biscuits left in the store for any future occupants.

We moved north without any serious problems for two or three days covering about twenty five miles a day, but it was hot and tiring. As we moved further north the local people were friendly and willingly gave us fruit and filled our water bottles, although we had nothing to give them in payment. On the third or fourth day we came across a stationary train with troops onboard. The train had been damaged and ad hoc repairs were being carried out. We were given a hot meal and offered a lift to Myitkyina, which we gladly accepted. The carriage we moved into was occupied by patients suffering from malaria, various other fevers and half a dozen slightly wounded men, plus two QARANCs (Queen Alexandra's Royal Army Nursing Corps) and two male attendants. One man was completely covered with brilliant red scales from head to foot. The rest of the train, five or six carriages, was filled with Venereal Disease patients including Officers. One of the male medic attendants told me that the only medication he had for the VD patients was methylated spirits and that many of his patients were in a very bad state. Some had ulcers large enough to accommodate a billiard ball. I understood that the train had been stopped on several occasions because of blockages being placed on the lines, presumably by Burmese friendly to the Japanese. During our stay on the train, for the best part of two days, we were twice attacked by Japanese planes, but with little damage and no casualties. The pilots were probably running short of ammunition or were in a hurry to get back to base. We arrived at Myitkyina airfield which was enormously crowded with civilians and a few military, all hoping to be evacuated to India. We were told the airfield was to be abandoned in the very near future. Dakota planes were being used for the evacuation and several would be arriving each day. A young Sikh Captain with a section of Sikh troops was responsible for the selection of passengers for evacuation. He had my sympathy; what a duty! On the day we arrived two Dakota's touched down, there was an immediate undisciplined rush to the planes but somehow the young Captain and his men managed, somewhat roughly, to load up their human cargo and get the planes airborne. During the next few days, seeing planes arrive and take off, our small party was becoming resigned to having to make a decision regarding walking out to India. Eventually, we realised that we could not put off making a decision much longer and were on the point of giving up hope and making plans for our walk out on foot when the Sikh Captain informed us that he was expecting several Dakota's early next morning and that we should be ready to depart. It was late in the afternoon when they arrived and, prior to emplaning all rifles, ammunition, equipment and baggage had to be discarded; space was too valuable. The planes were quickly filled to capacity, but our first attempt to take off was a failure and we were told to crowd together as close as possible towards the front of the plane. Fortunately, our second attempt to take off was successful. The plane flew low over the jungle, a sitting duck for any marauding Japanese planes. This was my very first journey in a plane. I was very surprised how clear paths and tracks could be seen from the air and thought of the many times I had camouflaged myself, possibly to no avail. We landed at an airfield in Assam where we were given a warm welcome and a well cooked hot meal. A short time later we were put into rail goods wagons for evacuation to the south. We had plenty of room to stretch out on the metal floors, but no bedding, which was of no concern to us as we had not had any for several months. The slightly wounded were accommodated in more comfortable carriages. My leg and fingers were swollen, dirty and bloody, the flies were a nuisance and I had a fever. All I wanted was to relax and sleep, and sleep...

Two or three days later I awoke when the train stopped at Lucknow. I was in a very comfortable train with lots of other soldiers and, I had no recollection of being moved from the original train or of anything that took place during the whole journey. There were ferries to cross, different gauge lines, and the distance must have been over 1,200 miles. The train stopped at Lucknow where the more seriously wounded were being transferred to the British Medical Hospital, Lucknow (BMH). Because of my legs and fever, I was also moved to the BMH. I was put in a small, isolated bedroom for one and told that a doctor would be along in a short while. The bed looked so clean and so neat that I considered myself to be too filthy to even sit on it; so I lay on the floor. I was not there very long before an army doctor and a male nurse came in. They took my temperature, which was 104F, checked me over, cleaned the holes in my leg - no fly eggs or maggots. They then gave me some pills and said that I was being put into the fever ward. I was still being documented when to my utter astonishment, Sheleagh with my son Michael and a welfare lady walked in. I knew that Sheleagh had been evacuated to India but I had not the slightest idea that she was in Lucknow -what a surprise! The welfare had been checking daily the names of personnel listed on trains arriving in Lucknow and had found my name on the list. The welfare lady suggested that if the doctor agreed, I could be accommodated with Sheleagh. The doctor, who was uncertain of the cause of my fever, agreed that if I took the pills that he gave to Sheleagh and kept in touch with the hospital, it would be OK. The welfare lady took us in her own car saying that she would call in at her bungalow and make me a cold drink. The bungalow was air-conditioned and situated in surrounding green gardens. After covering a large easy chair with a very large towel, for me to sit in, she gave me the most refreshing, tasty and most welcome drink that I have ever had, or ever have had since. Her daughter, about 17/18 years of age, dressed all in white, walked or floated into the room and I really thought that I was dreaming, or dead and that she was an angel.

Sheleagh's accommodation was a very large house (Moti Mahal) surrounded by large well kept gardens. About twenty of the Gloucester and KOYLI wives, all recently evacuated from Burma, were also accommodated there. I had a very refreshing but painful bath with two changes of water. This was my first bath, or good wash, since leaving Yenangyaung in March and then into a comfortable bed where I slept for the best part of two days. My filthy shirt and shorts were beyond washing and were dumped. Sheleagh bought me, for I had no money, new KD and after four or five days she and I took a Tonga into town where we had the good meal she had promised me. I still had my fever and my legs were painful, especially wearing slacks, but I had been looking forward to a nice quiet meal, just the two of us. Sadly, it was not to be for I was not up to it. The ride in the Tonga had upset me, I fiddled with the food, eating very little but, several months later we did enjoy a good meal and a night out together in Lucknow.

After about a week in Moti Mahal, I was moved to a hospital in Murree, in the cool Himalayas. Sheleagh and my son Michael were moved with several of the other wives to Upper Topa, also in the Himalayas and a few miles from Murree. I was in a party of about twenty men consisting of KOYLI, Gloucester's and the Duke of Wellington's, ordered to be moved to the hospital in Murree. We had a comfortable journey travelling 2nd Class about 700 miles to Rawalpindi passing through Delhi, Amritsar and Lahore in the foothills of the Himalayas. Rawalpindi is a little cooler than Lucknow and was dusty and crowded with lots of heavily laden bullock carts, donkeys and camels all moving at a slow leisurely pace. Heaps of mangoes and lychees were piled at the roadside awaiting transportation. After waiting on the train for about an hour, we were put into ambulances and commenced our journey of forty or fifty miles to Murree. The road was tortuous, narrow and steep, full of pot-holes and with innumerable hair-pin bends. Steep rock on one side of the road, and a small wall of dry stone about eighteen inches high on the other giving no protection to a drop of several thousands of feet - more of a guide and warning to the driver to keep to the centre of the road. We had two or three very welcome halts for a drink and a sandwich and to allow the engine of the ambulances to cool down. The scenery was truly magnificent, green and serene stretching to the horizon with rarely any sign of habitation. It was cool and the air was clean and fresh, it was good. I am not certain how long the journey took, but it must have been close to four hours. On arrival at the hospital in the late evening I was given a quick check-up, had a very enjoyable shower then assigned a bed with clean white sheets and a mosquito net. I slept solidly until late next morning. I was given another medical check, a little more thorough than the night before. My temperature was still close to 104 degrees Fahrenheit and my legs were painful and ulcerated. Although my wrist and fingers were quite swollen they were not painful. Actually, I felt quite well, but weak and knackered.

The hospital was extremely clean, with a perfect view of the Himalayas and the air coming through the windows was cool and sweet. I was given three hot meals a day, generally chicken followed by jelly and fresh cream, plenty of fresh fruit and a pint of milk-stout every day. I was thin and skinny, weighing about eight stone, very tense and up-tight. The nurses were cheerful, efficient and very helpful. I ate all the food given to me and for the first week or so, slept soundly between meals. Life was good and very comfortable. I did have difficulty in casting out the shadows of the past few months and felt guilty of this comfort when many of my friends were dead; many of them unburied and left to the vultures. I was in hospital for four weeks. Sheleagh visited me twice during my stay in hospital. It being an extremely difficult journey of six or seven miles on horseback, plus she had to get someone to accompany her, it not being safe for a woman to travel on her own. She insisted on paying for her escort, a soldier and his horse, and I was extremely pleased to see her and to know that she and Michael were well and safely settled in Upper Topa. I was very worried about her making such a hazardous and dangerous journey and concerned that she should arrive back at Upper Topa before dark. There were no street lights, it was dangerous in daylight and very much more so in the dark; there were wild animals in the surrounding hills, such as hyenas, jackals and the odd panther. There was no means of informing me that she had got home safely. After about two weeks in hospital, I slowly began to put on weight, the ulcers on my legs felt and looked much better but my fever and temperature still remained high. I was never told which particular fever it was and I don't think the doctors knew.

After four very comfortable, and well fed, weeks, I was discharged from hospital and given four weeks leave, which I spent with Sheleagh in Upper Topa. I made the journey on horseback since I could never have made it on foot. I most sincerely thanked the nurses who had looked after me for they had been so thoughtful, cheerful and efficient in returning me back to health. When I left them, my thoughts went back to that other nurse of 'long ago' in another world of smoke and death - Yenangyaung. I was truly in deep debt to these nurses; the latter will never fade from my memory. I spent four lazy weeks in Upper Topa, a smart hill-station with accommodation perched precariously on the hillside, a small but well stocked bazaar and a large Church of England church. The congregation on a Sunday evening consisted of the Padre, his wife and barely a handful of friends. A great pity because it was such a beautiful church. I went on two occasions. The view from this accommodation was absolutely marvellous.

The ulcers on my legs quickly healed, but I could not walk very far without resting, which meant that family walks were very restricted. Sheleagh had adjusted magnificently to her new life and new responsibilities in a new and strange environment amongst strangers, and having a young baby only a few months old while having to cope with household problems etc. She was young, and to a great extent had led a very sheltered and well organised life whilst in Burma. It was extremely worrying for her when Michael contracted Enteritis. It was 'touch and go' whether he would recover from it; five or six other children did die, including a set of twins. It was due to Sheleagh's nursing and care that he successfully recovered. One day we were very surprised when a close and old friend, 'Nutty Taylor' walked in; he was on convalescent leave in Murree recovering from malaria. He stayed with us for a couple of very enjoyable days. We had lots to talk about and I was very glad to see that he had managed to safely get out of Burma. The last time I had seen him was when he was in the lead Platoon and walking straight towards a Japanese machine-gun emplacement. On completion of my leave I was ordered to report to a re-enforcement unit in Lucknow. It was a sad parting, but at least I knew that Sheleagh and Michael were safely out of danger. We had no idea when we would meet again.

A wooden seat in a rickety old bus for about forty miles and I arrived in Rawalpindi, with a bruised and aching backside. A comfortable soft leather bunk, all to myself, in a 2nd Class carriage for 700 miles and I was in Lucknow. The unit to which I had been posted was accommodated in large brick-built barrack blocks; each block accommodated about a hundred men. The strength of the unit must have been well over a thousand men, all waiting to be returned to their units, or for medical re-grading, or for discipline purposes. It was disorganised with very little discipline, lots of drunkenness and very few duties or work. In general I felt quite fit, but if I walked more than 300 yards I felt knackered. I soon became very bored and wanted to do something. After two extremely boring weeks I was given a Medical Board and graded B1 for three months. I contacted the SSO (Station Staff Officer), a Captain, and asked him if there was any type of appointment available that would give me something to do for the next three months. I gave him a quick resume of my army service and was very surprised when he offered me the vacant appointment of running the Station Mobilisation Stores. I told him that I had very little knowledge of store keeping, but he assured me that I would find it easy and I accepted with some doubts. He took me in a Tonga to the stores, which were about a mile away telling me to keep a record of all my journeys by Tonga and that he would refund the cost. The stores consisted of a small office and six very large barrack blocks, filled to capacity with every item that a newly raised unit would require. I was impressed at the magnitude of the stores. What about the accounting? I was more than a little perturbed, but I had nothing to worry about; all accounting was done in AB (A4 lined books with perpendicular columns - date, item, quantity, receipt in, receipt out and balance in stock; very simple). The Senior Staff Officer told me to be particularly careful when issuing pocket watches for Officers. He was unconcerned in respect of any other items.

The authorised establishment was one Warrant Officer, one British Corporal, two Naiks and six Sepoys. I was very busy for the next two weeks familiarising myself with the issue and receipt of stores and the multitude of the stores in the barrack blocks. When I required them I was given any number of fatigue parties, and as many bullock carts as I considered necessary. The two Naiks from the Royal Indian Army Service Corps (RIASC) were very reliable and most efficient, both speaking perfect English. I got to like them and trusted them completely. When dealing with the British troops I made sure the two Naiks were never insulted or abused. After three or four weeks the system became routine and I had no problems, and I gave the Senior Staff Officer (SSO) no problems. I had got myself a very cushy job.

In late October, or early November, Sheleagh and Michael arrived from Upper Topa. With the help of the SSO I had managed to give them one of the best available married quarters, which I had moved into a few days prior to their arrival. It was wonderful to be together again. We had that celebration meal which we had promised ourselves many months before. Once again Sheleagh adjusted easily and quickly into new surroundings and new problems. After about three interesting months in the Mob Store I was relieved by the official Warrant Officer from the RIASC. The SSO thanked me for filling the vacancy and offered me an appointment in the Brigade Office. I had never worked in an office, but he said not to worry and was sure that I would adjust. I accepted; anything to keep me out of the RU. He gave me seven days leave - we were getting quite friendly.

I duly reported to the Brigade HQ, a large building surrounded by a strong metal fence, with some trepidation. After my identity was carefully checked I was shown into G Branch, where there was a vacancy for a Sergeant. The Chief Clerk was a WO1, (Warrant Officer 1) a WO11 from the Education Corps dealt with intelligence gathering, a Corporal from the Royal Signals dealt with the training of pigeons, A Sergeant in the WACI did shorthand and typing. 'G' Branch dealt with security training, intelligence gathering, security of information, identity cards for Officers etc. The GSO 111 was a Captain Lunzer, who was an ex-overseas salesman for a type-writer company. The Brigade Major was Major Leverson-Gower. My first week was mainly spent checking details on Officers Identity Cards and assisting the Chief Clerk in general. I found everyone in the Branch very helpful and friendly. I took a keen interest in everything that was going on and was always eager to assist in any possible way. I wanted to learn. During the whole of my service in the KOYLI, I had never had the opportunity to see, or to read, any sort of army manuals or regulations. Here, where the shelves were stacked high with all types of manuals and regulations, and all available to me, I regularly stayed in the office for an hour or so, after the others had left, and taught myself to type. When I showed an interest in shorthand, the WACI Sergeant loaned me a book about it and later, I volunteered to stay with the Chief Clerk whenever he was detailed for night duty.

Christmas 1942 came and passed, almost unnoticed. I was with my wife and son, what more could I ask or wish for. Over the next two or three weeks Sheleagh and I visited several places of interest, such as the Residency, where British troops were besieged during the Indian mutiny of 1856, Moti Mahal (Pearl Palace), which Sheleagh knew quite well but I had only a very hazy recollection of; La Martiniere College, built by a French General in 1845 with its beautiful lake, monuments and green gardens. Dilkusha Kothi Palace, built by the Murghals and connected to the mutiny and several other less significant monuments depicting the British Raj. We had some quite enjoyable meals in the city, the odd dance and social evenings in the Mess. My old friend, Nutty Taylor had been transferred to the hospital in Lucknow, he had malaria on the brain and was placed on the dangerously ill list and was not expected to live. He looked very pale, sick and thin but very pleased to see me, we had been very close friends in Maymyo. I thought he was going to die since not many patients ever recovered from this particular strain of malaria. I was very surprised, and relieved, when he recovered. There were several other KOYLI soldiers in the hospital suffering from wounds and a variety of fevers, and six or seven in the Military prison serving sentences for one to ten years for various disciplinary reasons.

I attended a Medical Board in late February/early March and told the board that I considered myself fit and well. After a short and quick routine check, I was regarded as fit for all duties. I informed the Brigade Major of my change in medical grading, anticipating that I would be quickly returned to my Battalion, which was being reorganised, re-equipped and re-enforced in Delhi. I had enjoyed the last three or four months (freedom from bullshit and drill), but realised that now being fit, I was duty bound to report back to my Battalion. I had found my time in the Brigade Office very interesting and enlightening. I had taken a keen interest in all aspects of the work being done and had become quite competent in taking over some small but responsible duties. I had learned much about army procedures, ranks and formations. The Brigade Major, an elderly and approachable person, told me that I had two options - be posted back to my Battalion, or be seconded as a clerk to a Brigade office. If I decided on the latter, I would keep my rank and that he would give me a good recommendation that I be posted to a more active Brigade or formation, most probably in Assam. He gave me a few days to make up my mind. After seriously discussing the options with my brother David, who was still with the Battalion and told me it was still in a disorganised mess and very much under strength, and the memory of Captain (ex RSM) Miller who had told me at Toksan to "not give him the shits"; of the young and green 2nd Lieutenant who had insisted that we carry full sized spades when going into close combat attack; I decided on secondment. My son Sidney was born on the 31st March in the Lucknow Military Hospital and I was very fortunate in being able to organise his Christening prior to my expected posting. I stayed in Lucknow until mid April when I received a posting order to report to 14/24 MFO in Calcutta. Another sad parting; I hated leaving Sheleagh and the two children, but she was safe and among friends. We had no idea when or where we would meet again.

In May 1943 I was given a rail warrant for a 2nd Class ticket and had a very comfortable journey on the Bombay to Calcutta Mail train. It had priority over all other trains, no waiting on side-lines as per troop trains. It was about 1,250 miles to Calcutta and I think it took close on the best part of two days to reach there. Rail traffic, munitions, armour, tanks, vehicles and personnel were extremely heavy; all moving east. I arrived at Howrah, the main rail station to the west of Calcutta and to the west of the river Houghly, clean, fed and refreshed. Howrah had a very large and busy station which was extremely crowded with military and civilians, the civilians appeared to be in a great hurry to move out because of a recent Japanese air raid on the docks. I managed to obtain a lift in a 15 cwt truck going to Fort William, south of the river, where I reported for duty. I was told that my posting was to 14 MFO, a unit of a newly formed Brigade based in Barrackpore, the MFO being based in Howrah, and that I would be billeted in West Howrah. I had been to Calcutta on several occasions in the 30's, but I was in for a few surprises and disappointments. I had expected to be posted to a Brigade HQ in the Arakan or Assam area, there being a very large number of such HQ's being formed at this time.

My billet was a long low brick building with about eight rooms on the ground floor and eight on the first floor. Each room being about seven feet by seven feet, had one small window, a small chair and one iron bed, 2ft 6in wide with a coir mattress and no fans! One ground floor room was used as a toilet, a single large bucket, and one water tap for washing and drinking, the water being of doubtful quality and a dubious colour. An open sewer ran down the street in front of the billet, the street itself being washed down daily with river water from street's hydrants. The toilet bucket quickly filled and spilled over onto the floor and after about a fortnight it was so battered it was not possible to operate the door. The mosquitoes were large and thirsty. The fifteen or so occupants were WO's and NCO's from various units and formations in Calcutta.

After about two weeks, I queried the sanitation situation with the medical authorities who readily agreed that the billets were most unsuitable. We were moved into a much larger and cleaner billet in Kali Tagore Street in Calcutta. This was a large three storied brick building, with a centre well about fifteen feet square and open from the ground floor to the roof for ventilation. About fifty rooms were built around the well with the flat roof giving a marvellous view of Calcutta. The accommodation was for about fifty WO's and NCO's working in various Headquarters. Calcutta was awash with troops in preparation for the defence of Assam and for the offensive in the Arakan.

The unit to which I was posted was commanded by an Indian Captain by the name of Mascarinas. He had been educated in England, keen on cricket, and was a real gentleman, but not long in the army. The unit consisted of myself, the only European, four Naiks (Corporals), three Sepoy clerks and ten Sepoy craftsmen, plus the authority to employ as many Coolies as necessary. All the military could speak English, but they did not consist of any Sikhs, Bengalis or Tamils. I had to familiarise myself regarding their religion, pay, rations, medics, inoculations etc. The Captain drew the Imprest Account and enjoyed paying out the military, but left the Coolies to me - a messy job, two thumb prints per Coolie, generally about fifty of them. Our main work was to check all rail wagons arriving in Howrah from the west and unload all those destined for units in and around twenty miles of Calcutta. We also had to inform the units regarding collection, and complete the necessary paperwork, which was very basic and simple. Other rail wagons destined for Assam and the Arakan areas were arranged for immediate onward movement. Similar RAF and American units to ours were also located close by. An American Liaison Sergeant by the name 'Lucky' shared my office.

This was not what I expected, which was an appointment with an active field Brigade. I began to doubt whether I had made the right decision to opt for secondment as against returning to my unit, at present in Delhi. My duties were new to me, interesting, quite a lot of it outdoors and it kept me busy. There were no parades, inspections and no-bullshit. I made a special effort to get to know my IOR's (Indian Other Ranks), their homes, families, military service etc and after my recent experiences in Burma I had formed a great respect for the Indian soldier. I ensured they were given their full entitlement of rations, suitable accommodation and treated with respect when dealing with BOR's, (British Other Ranks) which on occasions was difficult because of the ignorance of the BOR's. Calcutta was awash with troops, British, American, African and Indian. (I was surprised how roughly the black American troops were handled by the white American Military Police). Supplies of armour and equipment for the troops in Assam and the Arakan, was pouring into Calcutta by air, sea, rail and road. To add to the hectic, busy and overcrowded situation there was a very serious outbreak of smallpox, with claims of illegal distribution of the serum. There was also a very severe famine throughout Bengal which affected the supply of food into the city. Women and children were dying in the streets in large numbers; the dead often being left on the streets for up to two days before being removed. I saw many pitiful sights, especially of dying breast-feeding mothers with other children. It was a punishable military offence to give them food on the grounds that it would encourage more to come to the city and spread disease to the army. The local roadside stall holders declined to help their own people! I well remember seeing the body of a Hindu who had committed suicide on the railway line quite close to the main line platform, his body was completely cut in half. It remained there in the heat of the day, covered in flies for the best part of two days before being removed.

Calcutta was a truly crowded, dirty, busy and a thriving city with indescribable problems.

I had a severe attack of Dengue fever in late 1943 which lasted for about four days and left me very weak in the legs for about a week. On several occasions I took the opportunity to accompany the unit Representative, with the stores, back to their area in the Arakan. This gave me a break from the routine in Calcutta and a change of scenery. I did the same on the Imphal line. On one of the Arakan trips I noticed signs of hurried with-drawls. I wondered if there had been another Burma strategic with-drawl, but I never got to know. The weeks and months of 1944 quickly passed and Christmas was just another day.

In early May 1945, I managed to get a few days leave to Lucknow. I found a big change in the family, especially in Sidney who was coming up to two years of age and announced my arrival in Urdu. Michael had grown quite a lot and Sheleagh looked a little thin but beautiful. It was wonderful to see and meet them again. I had collected quite a number of presents for them over the last year which they enjoyed opening. We managed to go to the cinema a couple of times and Sheleagh's mother, who had joined the ATS and lived on the same married quarters block, looked after the boys. I enjoyed every minute of my short stay in Lucknow and left completely assured that my family was safe, comfortable and well looked after by the military authorities.

Whilst in Lucknow I had met my brother David who was also on leave in Lucknow where his wife was accommodated. We had lots to talk about. The Battalion was still in Delhi, being brought up to strength, re-armed and retrained and I had been right to opt for secondment. We never met again. The future was beginning to look much brighter. The war in Europe appeared to be coming to an end. The Japanese in Burma were in full retreat, Mandalay had been taken, the Arakan was almost cleared and our troops were converging on Rangoon. The Yanks were thrashing the Japanese in the Pacific, but what was my future? I would have to wait and see. Rangoon was taken on 1st May 1945 and in July I was informed that I and my family would be repatriated to the UK. This was quite a shock. I was pleased, but at the same time disappointed as I would have liked to have gone back into northern Burma for at least a few weeks. It was the government's policy that personnel with the longest service in the east would be given priority in repatriation to the UK. I had been in the East for over thirteen years. It took me no more than a couple of days to hand over my duties, pack my kit-bag and be on my way to Lucknow. Sheleagh was extremely surprised to see me, and still more surprised when I told her that we would be on our way to England within the next two weeks. We didn't have much in the way of heavy baggage, Sheleagh's sewing machine being the heaviest item, but we did have six good American made blankets and six cotton sheets, plus a lot of Sheleagh's dresses which she had sewn herself. We quickly bought warm clothing and several pairs of new shoes for all the family. We also packed lots of tinned salmon, bully beef, fruit and cigarettes. I thought that these items would, one way or another help us to adjust to the rationing in the UK. Sheleagh said good-bye to the friends she had made whilst in Lucknow and we were on our way to Deolalli, a camp a few miles from Bombay. The camp, a forming camp for personnel prior to their embarkation from Bombay, was very basic. The food was only just above starvation level and very basic which meant that it was necessary to supplement it from a nearby dirty and dodgy bazaar. The weather was dry and hot, the temperature being well over 100*F. It was too hot to sleep in the huts provided, so we slept on the open Miadan. Fortunately, we only stayed in Deolalli for three days before moving to Bombay and boarding the good ship Multan.

On board the Multan Sheleagh shared a cabin with three other wives and their four children. It was very crowded, noisy, bitchy, and with lots of arguments over dirty and wet napkins. Sheleagh disliked it intensely and spent every minute she possibly could on a higher deck. I was accommodated on a troop deck, three decks below the water-line, where on occasion the temperature reached 156*F, and the smell was awful. The food on the

Multan consisted mainly of fish, which was plentiful and well cooked, but there was a complete lack of vegetables and fruit which resulted in nearly every child going down with a type of scurvy and boils. In our family Sheleagh got two nasty looking boils on her neck, Michael and Sidney got boils on their necks and their backs and I got a carbuncle two weeks after we landed in the UK, which gave birth to three boils and left an ugly looking crater in my neck. The large variety of fish swimming alongside the ship, from sinister looking sharks, porpoise, coloured and flying fish, fascinated Michael and Sidney. They never got tired of watching them and on the whole it was not a pleasant voyage, the ship was vastly overcrowded, but this was understandable since shipping space was just not available. We were very lucky to get a berth since we could have been waiting for another year or so. The 'Multan' berthed in Greenock in Scotland in August 1945. Movement controllers had boarded the ship earlier in the day and were in possession of our family details. They were very helpful and quickly arranged for our onward movement. They gave us a choice of military stations for Married Quarters in Catterick, Taunton, Aldershot, Winchester and Colchester, all of which were unfamiliar to me. We settled for Colchester and were given the necessary warrants plus, most importantly, four weeks leave. They also arranged for our heavy baggage in the ship's hold to be transported to Colchester. Disembarkation of the 2,000 troops was truly chaotic since they were very impatient to get off the ship with or without documentation.

We had a small end compartment on the train, which consisted of a four-seater padded bench that was comfortable, small and private. A bevy of WVS ladies gave us some very welcome tea and biscuits prior to the train moving off. Michael and Sidney slept on the bench while Sheleagh and I slept on the floor for we were all very, very, tired. Next morning, a little refreshed, we began to take more interest in the view of the countryside. It was all new to Sheleagh and the boys. At one of the stops, we managed to get some tea and biscuits, thanks again to the WVS. It was a long and tiring journey, especially for the boys. We arrived at Kings Cross Station mid-afternoon and were met by a member of the MC and taken by truck over to Liverpool Street station. I was completely shocked by the amount of destruction and desolation caused by enemy bombing. Another two hour journey by rail and we arrived at our final destination, Colchester. It was a strange and new situation for all of us. We were in a country ravaged by six years of war with empty stores and shops, and coupons required for every basic need. We had arrived in Colchester late on a Friday afternoon when every Government office was closed, which meant we had to wait until Monday before we could collect the all important dockets and coupons. The married quarter that I had taken over was sparsely furnished with one table and four fold flat chairs, four single beds with coir mattresses and pillows, about twelve well worn thin blankets, a kettle and three cooking pans. No carpets or curtains - it did look a little bare. We went to the NAAFI, which was close by, where we purchased tea and sandwiches, not withstanding that we hadn't any coupons. I also borrowed four mugs, plates and some cooking utensils from the NAAFI. Saturday and Sunday was a little tough food wise, but the NAAFI was very helpful. We could not, and did not complain, it had been a devastating war and there must have been many, many people in much worse conditions than us. We were at the head of the queue on Monday morning for our coupons, dockets and ration books. My four weeks leave enabled me to ensure that Sheleagh and the boys were well settled in our new home and well versed in the complicated rationing and coupon system. I also arranged for her to receive a weekly allowance. Sheleagh adjusted magnificently to our new and strange situation. She made curtains and stair carpets from blankets I had obtained from the local unit Quarter Master who smoked - we had a considerable amount of cigarettes in our luggage. We also managed to arrange an amicable agreement with the local butcher, who liked the tea we had. By the time my leave had ended, Sheleagh and the boys had adjusted and settled down much better than I expected. A few days before my leave ended, I received an order to report to a Reinforcement Camp in Leeds.

On arrival in Leeds I was very surprised to find that the camp was actually a street of dilapidated terrace houses. Filthy and run down, doors and windows in a bad condition, the furniture consisted of 2ft 6in iron beds with coir mattresses and pillows, three very thin blankets and fold-flat chairs. The whole street had been taken over by the War Department only a few weeks earlier. They had been empty for a considerable time and had been severely vandalised. For the next few days, it was buckets, brushes, soap and water to clean up the accommodation and live like human beings, or do nothing and live like pigs. After a few days the house I shared with about ten other Sergeants began to look quite reasonable. A central cook-house produced fairly good meals in sufficient quantities. We were made very welcome in the city and given free tickets to the cinemas and theatres. I stayed in this makeshift accommodation for about three weeks, when orders were received that all Sergeants were to be moved to a Nissan Camp on the outskirts of the city. It took me less than two minutes to pack. My new camp, about two miles out of Leeds on a green hillside, was an unbelievable contrast to the camp I had just left. Nissan huts were well spaced out with flower gardens and providing accommodation for over a thousand WO's and NCO's from various Regiments, all waiting for de-mob or posting to a Regular unit if they still had Regular Service to complete. Duties were very few, one Muster parade in the morning at 9.00am to check for absentees and announce out-going postings. Again we were given free tickets by the City Council to cinemas and theatres and many individual invitations to dinners and private parties from a very friendly population. I spent about five weeks in this camp before receiving my next posting to Winchester, for duties in an Army Record Office. Ten other sergeants accompanied me.

I was very surprised on arrival in Winchester to notice the complete absence of young men in town - only old men. We were accommodated in Nissan huts in Bushfield Camp, on the outskirts of town. Our duties at the Record Office were to calculate the amount of Service, Pay and Leave in respect of WRAC being de-mobbed, repetitive but not boring. We had a hot mid-day meal at the Record Office, about which we said nothing and another hot meal at the camp on our return there about 6.00pm. I began to put on some much needed weight; a pint of King Alfred stout also helped. Our accommodation in the camp was clean and comfortable, and there were no parades or inspections. We were basically treated as a small independent unit, whose sole duty was at the Record Office. I managed to spend a week-end in Colchester with Sheleagh and the boys every week, from after duty on Friday to 9.00am on the Monday. I was in Winchester for just over five weeks, which I thoroughly enjoyed; accommodation was good, food good and plentiful, entertainment good, the locals friendly and I got to have week-ends with my family.

After five weeks of something like luxury, our party of ten was posted to Reading for work in the Royal Signals Record Office. Our accommodation was again in Nissan huts which were quite clean, well furnished and comfortable and about a mile outside the town. The food was good and plentiful, no parades, inspections or duties. Work in the Record Office was similar to that which we carried out in Winchester. The locals were friendly and the landlords of the public houses went out of their way to welcome us. I think they were all very pleased to see the troops coming home after five years of war. I didn't spend much time in Reading, preferring to visit the villages on the outskirts. The countryside was at its best, the air was clean and fresh and the scenery wonderful. I spent much of my off-duty time, wandering around the countryside. I was in Reading for about six weeks, but because of work, I only managed to visit the family in Colchester on four weekends.

Agra India 1935. Fred with Pith Hat,
David Second from right.

Agra india 1936. Fred 1st on Left 2nd Row. David Last on Right 2nd Row.

Four PRICES ; Sid, James, David, Fred.
Maymyo, Burma 1936

Band & Buglers. Changing of the Guard,
Maymyo, Upper Burma 1936
Fred and David on parade

Frederick Lloyd, Maymyo, Burma 1936. Lee Enfield rifle

Goteik Viaduct Burma 1936

Hockey team; Fred, Armstrong, Judd,
Moulds and Barrow Book, Schofield, Ackland.
Maymyo Burma 1936/7

Mandalay 1936. Two typical Barrack Blocks

My Barrack room in Maymyo, Burma 1936-7 and 1938-1940. Taken by B Vause in January '05

On the road to Khangi from Maymyo, Burma 1936 or 1939. 39/45 miles

Maymyo Burma 1936. Fred and David on parade

The Troopship Talamba.
Built in 1924 at Hebbun. Speed 16 Knots. Talamba is a town near Multan in Pakistan. The 2nd Bn KOYLI moved from Calcutta to Rangoon in Burma on her on March 1936. My brothers James, Sidney, David and myself were on board. The Talamba took part in picking up the survivors from the Battleship 'Prince of Wales' and the Battle Cruiser 'Repulse' sunk by the Japanese off Malaya on 10th Dec 1941. She was sunk by German action at the Sicily landings in September 1943.

Talamba; 2nd Bn KOYLI moved from Calcutta to Rangoon on her in March 1936. Jim, Sid, David and Fred all on board. Later picture - 3 funnels on ship

Typical building and transport in Maymyo 1936

Hockey Team; Band 2nd KOYLI, Maymyo Burma. Fred Back row extreme Left, David Back row three from Left. The Band team won the Bn. 'Scissors Cup' nearly every year.

Maymyo 1938/39. Bn. Buglers and Band

Maymyo 1938 (Band 2 KOYLI). Church parade. BandMaster JCJ Martin.

Maymyo 1938 (2nd KOYLI) Bn. Returning to Barracks from Church Parade. Officer Lt Vickers.

Fred & David Maymyo 1938/39 Burma.

Maymyo 1938 (2nd KOYLI). Mounted Colonel TB Butt, Capt Roberts (Adj)
Clarinet L/Cpl F Price, Bandsman F Plowman.

The Troopship 'Dilwara'.

The first purpose built Troopship in the 20th Century. Built in Glasgow in 1936 at a cost of £403,700. Speed 14 Knots. I travelled on her in 1938 from India to the UK.

HMT Dilwara 1938 FLP India to UK

David Allen, Frederick Lloyd Price.
Maymyo, Upper Burma 1939

'Fred serenading us'. Fred with Sax, Graham and David with Towels. Ashford in background. 1939 Maymyo Burma.

L to R Bandsmen Graham, David and Fred

Feb 10th 1941 - Marriage

Botanical Gardens Maymyo 1936/4

The River Sittang. Taken by B Vause January '05

Fred & Sheleagh Price, Murree Hills, India 1942

On the steps of Havelock, Lucknow. 1942.
Sheleagh & Fred

Upper Topa India 1942 (now Pakistan). David with Wendy, Fred with Michael. Hospital and convalescence

Fred Price (on leave) Havelock Lines, Lucknow 1944.

POST WAR, ROYAL ARMY SERVICE CORPS

My next posting was to an RASC Collection Unit in Tarporley, Cheshire where I spent autumn and a very cold winter, in a very cold Nissan hut. There were about fifteen occupants, Sergeants like myself and recently returned to the UK from the Far and Middle East and who felt the cold as much as I did. The total number of RASC personnel in the camp must have been close to 500, all impatiently waiting for de-mob or a posting to a Regular unit. I still had one year of my reserve service to complete, it looked like a long and boring one. To avoid the bullshit, parades and guards, I volunteered to be in charge of the escort for the collection and despatch of deserters to and from prisons in Central and Southern England. This gave me the opportunity to spend quite a number of weekends with the family in Colchester. Although Sheleagh and the boys had settled down quite well, I was still a little concerned about their situation. I escorted many odd prisoners, some meek and frightened, and some big mean and angry who needed to be permanently handcuffed, even when going to the toilet. I met many dirty looks from civilian passengers when I handcuffed the prisoners. On the other hand,

I took them to the Pub for a drink, before delivering them into prison. On one occasion, collecting an AWOL (absent without leave) from Chelmsford Police Station, I allowed him to spend the night at home with his wife prior to returning him to his unit. I spent that night in Colchester with my family. Many prisoners did escape from their escorts, but never from mine. Although I spent a considerable amount of time on escort duties, with many additional weekends with my family, I still found time in the camp boring and depressing. Christmas 1945 was a welcome break, the camp practically closed down, except for a small security section, and everyone was given two weeks leave.

We were together as a family for two whole quiet, relaxed and happy weeks. Rationing of everything was extremely strict, the locals had put up with it for several years so how could we comment or question it. Christmas came along very quietly, no cards, no presents or sweets, but we were together, healthy and much better off in many respects than lots of other families. I managed, after much searching around the local villages, to buy a skinny, balding, half dead chicken from a sympathetic old lady who had a small derelict chicken-run and a few very elderly chickens. I was greatly concerned that it might die before I reached home and Sheleagh would never have cooked it; she would have thought it had died of old age or disease. I need not have worried, Sheleagh plucked and cooked it and we had a feast. Never had chicken tasted so good, and never had bones been picked so clean. My two weeks leave quickly passed and with that I was back in the cold Nissan hut in Tarporley.

The furnishing of the hut consisted of a considerable amount of wooden fittings such as, rifle racks, hooks and shelving, which we considered surplus to requirements! Gradually, over the next few weeks I spent in Tarporley, this surplus was whittled down to the absolute minimum - it kept us from freezing to death. No disciplinary action was taken against the occupants, but everyone was charged with the refurbishment. I was very pleased when I received orders to report for permanent duty to an RASC Armoured Regiment in Blackdown. What a strange posting, but anything was better than Tarporley. My knowledge of armour was very limited, I was more accustomed to mules, AT and bullock carts, I didn't even have a driving licence. I was surprised at the size of the camp and the number of units stationed there. I spent my first few days reconnoitring the unit area, identifying and familiarising myself with the masses of vehicles, tanks (large and small), armoured transporters, trucks, jeeps and motor cycles. I thought to myself that the replacement of components for this vast array of vehicles must be enormous, and would I be involved? Fortunately, the Regiment was not very active and did very little if any training. It had recently returned to the UK from Germany and was actually being run-down from its war establishment and a considerable number of its personnel were taking long over-due leave. After dreaming of masses of armoured tanks for about a week, I was asked to take over the unit's treasury and rationing department. I was told that it was at present hopelessly in a mess because of large under-withdrawals of some items and over-drawing of rations. The unit had been admonished for its inefficient accounting by District HQ. I agreed the appointment; anything to take me from dreaming about those tanks.

I took over a small office and its three clerks and was shocked to find that none of the Ration Manuals and directives had been amended or updated. I visited the local CSD (central supply depot) and the main Supply depot in Aldershot where they were very helpful and, after a long discussion, agreed to call it quits in respect of the under and over with-drawls. I could start off with a clean sheet and I had made two very useful contacts with men of my age and service. They also gave me the latest and up-to-date regulations on rations and rationing. I ensured that I was given, from Battalion HQ, accurate daily strengths of the Battalion and the inward and outward movement of personnel. I also obtained the accurate daily strengths of the Messes; Officers, WO's, NCO's, ATS ([Women's] Auxiliary Territorial Service) and other ranks. With daily accurate strengths, the paperwork was easy and, within less than three weeks everything was running smoothly with accurate demands being submitted on time to the Supply Depots. The Messes were able to confidently provide regular daily standard meals. The ATS Mess was particularly pleased as many of the additional items, milk, cocoa and cheese etc, for young growing girls, had never been fully demanded. I squeezed every additional ration possible out of the Supply Depots. The CO congratulated me on a job well done.

On the whole I enjoyed my time in Blackdown. No parades, guards, fatigues or bull, in a wonderful part of the country surrounded with unspoiled villages with rural pubs. My accommodation was a comfortable two roomed bunk at the end of a large barrack block holding about fifty young National Service recruits. I especially remember one particular Friday afternoon when the recruits were impatiently waiting to depart on weekend passes, when a fairly loud explosion occurred in the toilets. A soldier settling down on the throne had his testicle and penis severely burned and bruised. It looked, and must have been, very painful. Fortunately, nothing was missing. I sent him, with an escort in a vehicle to the hospital. Apparently, someone had placed an explosive device under the toilet seat. No-one owned up. I had all the windows closed and the door locked and informed everyone that no passes would be allowed until the culprit owned up, that I would keep them there all day and night if necessary. After about an hour, a very tearful and frightened young recruit, looking more like a young girl than a man, came forward and pleaded guilty. He handed me a handful of grenade detonators; he thought they were some sort of cracker. I explained to everyone, their purpose, how dangerous they were, and how very lucky it was that no-one had lost any fingers or suffered a more serious injury. I let them all, except the bomber, go on their week-end pass. I told the bomber that he was confined to barracks until I knew of the extent of the injury to his victim. Fortunately, he was not admitted to hospital but placed on the daily sick check parade. He walked with a peculiar limp for the next week or so. I handed in the tin of detonators to the ammunition store and told the bomber that he was very lucky that I was not taking disciplinary action against him. He was very young and very scared - I let him go on his week-end pass. I was stationed in Blackdown for about ten weeks and was hoping to complete my Colour Service of about one year there, but it was not to be. I was given a posting order to report to the RASC Training Centre, in a Brigadier's command in Aldershot. I knew that Aldershot was probably the largest military station in the UK - it looked like parades and bull for my last year in the Army. I left Blackdown with trepidation on a Sunday afternoon and booked myself into the WO's and Sergeants Mess in

Aldershot, to ensure that I would be on the spot for my interview on the Monday morning. I was duly interviewed by a Major Pooley and informed of the duties and position that I would be given. Basically, I was to be in charge of the A/Q Branch of the HQ RASC Training Centre.

ALDERSHOT 1946 TO 1953

My staff consisted of ten clerks, Corporals and below -Regulars and National Service men, all of them shorthand writers. I was very relieved to know that I would be attached to Training Battalion RASC, and for administrative purposes - no parades or Battalion duties. The HQ Staff consisted of a Brigadier, a Colonel, four Majors, four Captains, one WO1, one WO2 and two Sergeants. The two WO's had spent all their wartime service in the Aldershot area. I was very comfortable in the Mess and quickly adjusted to the office routine. It was very fortunate that I had taught myself the basics of shorthand whilst in Lucknow during my convalescence in 1942/3. I now had to take it more seriously. Major Pooley, head of A/Q Branch, suggested it would be to my benefit if I went to No2 training Battalion RASC, in Blackdown on a two week Clerical Course in shorthand for new entrants to the RASC. I was still basically an infantryman. I enjoyed the break and quickly realised how little I knew about the RASC, its organisation and its enormous commitment to the Army.

After about six weeks in Aldershot I managed to obtain Married Quarters for my family. Sheleagh was very pleased and it only took a couple of days to pack up our meagre belongings and move to Aldershot.

Sheleagh thought the new Married Quarters were dirty, which disappointed me since I had been cleaning it every night for about a week. It had accommodated Italian POW's prior to my taking it over. Sheleagh and the boys soon settled down to their new surroundings and life in a Military Station and we were together again as a family. There were excellent sporting facilities in Aldershot. Every unit had its own gymnasium, football, rugby, hockey and cricket grounds and tennis courts. I soon became a member of the No1 RASC Training Battalion hockey team, which won, or were runners-up, of Battalion, District and Command Competitions for the next six years. I became a regular member of the RASC's hockey team, which was formed from the best hockey players in the UK and Germany. I also became a member of the Fleet hockey club, a small village close to Aldershot. I was beginning to enjoy my life in Aldershot, and so were Sheleagh and the boys. My Colour and Reserve Service was coming to an end in February 1947 and I decided it was not the right time to leave the Army. I signed on to increase my Colour Service for ten years, with the option of terminating after each three year period.

I now considered my career more seriously with a view to improving my prospects of promotion. For the last two years my only thoughts had been to leave the Army at the first opportunity, but Major Pooley was a great help and arranged for me to attend a Chief Clerks Course at Blackdown. For three weeks I studied all types of documentation used in the Army and various units in the RASC, their ranks and appointments, from Private to General, their establishments and worldwide commitments. I asked to be tested for Shorthand (100 words a minute) which was agreed. I obtained a good Pass Report on the Main Course and a Pass Commendation on the clarity of my Shorthand. For the last few months, Sheleagh had been reading to me, testing my Shorthand, every night at speeds well over 100 words per minute. I had also taken a civilian correspondence course with Pitman's, hence my confidence in passing the Army test. War-time ranks were coming to an end in the late 1940's and early 1950's and qualifications were being strictly introduced for all current ranks. The main qualifications were Education, Weapons, Drill, Trade and Fitness. I had obtained a 1st Class Certificate of education in Agra in 1933. I took the test for Weapons and Drill at No. 1. Training Battalion, which was almost a waste of time but necessary. I had been a Marksman with the rifle for the whole of my military service since the age of sixteen, and was also proficient with all Infantry LMG's since the age of twenty. I also had personal experience with the use and maintenance of grenades. My trade as a Clerk required to be upgraded.

My third and last course at Blackdown was for three weeks in 1950. It was to qualify for the appointment of a B1 Superintendent Clerk; to be capable of taking over the responsibility of any office, in any formation, Brigade to GHQ, in the Army. I had to acquire a good knowledge of the Teeth, Supporting and supply Arms, their Establishment, Ranks and Appointments. I had to familiarise myself with the hundreds of abbreviations used in the field, until they became common usage. I worked hard, and for long hours, eventually taking the exam in March and was successful.

In 1950 I was, unknowingly, security vetted and cleared to see all Secret and Top Secret information and correspondence. I was also awarded the LSGC medal (Long Service and Good Conduct) in 1950, presented to me by the GSOI, Colonel T.E. Southwell, who I met again several years later when he was a Brigadier in Southern Command, and recommended me for accelerated promotion for a Commission. I was promoted to WO2 (Senior Quarter Master Sergeant) on the 1st October 1952. I was informed in January 1953 that I was to be posted to CRASC Malta in April. I had enjoyed my six years in Aldershot; especially the sport, and in particular the hockey and tennis, and also the fact that I had been able to avoid at least 95% of the Bull. I left Aldershot on the 13th April for Malta. Sheleagh and the boys joined me about seven weeks later.

Hockey Team - Officers & NCO's Wing RASC 1946/7; names on picture
b/row; Sgt F Mahon, Sgt F Price, Maj T Modesta, Capt F Hunter, 2nd/Lt A Dann.
f/row; BSM C Conway, Col J Mullington, Lt/Col E Hazelton (Capt), RSM C Rusell, Lt/Col J Rush, Maj J Kingsmill.

Hockey Team - Training Battalion RASC; names on picture
b/row; Maj W Bate, S/Sgt F Price, O/Cdt J Bruce, CQMS G Dean, 2nd/Lt A Dann, 2nd/Lt J Bartlett. Capt F Hunter, Lt/Col A MacDonald, Capt R Worth, Sgt F Mahon.

Fred & Sheleagh, Aldershot 1947

Fred two from left. Aldershot 1948

Field training. Fred on left. Aldershot 1948.

Hockey team; Officer's & NCO's Wing RASC, Aldershot 1948/9.
Fred front row third from right

Sgt's Mess, Aldershot 1948. Fred on left.

RASC Hockey Club 1948/9 Season (names on picture) b/row; Sgt Grant, S/Sgt Price, SSM Thompson, O/Cdt Carruthers, Cpl Wellington, QSMI Beadle. f/row; Capt C Bullough, SSM Osborne, Capt T Podesta, Maj R Worth, Maj J Bate, SSM Wilson, BSM Mahon.

Tidworth 1948. Jean, Ian, Joan, Sheleagh, Molly, Michael, Sid

Aldershot '48. Sheleagh Fred.

RASC Dance Aldershot 1949/50. Sheleagh & Fred

Aldershot 1950. Michael, Sheleagh,
Ian, Fred, Sidney.

Sheleagh Tidworth 1951/52

SQMS Fred Price, Aboukir Terrace, Aldershot 1951

Fred Aldershot '52

MALTA 13TH APRIL 1953 TO 17TH SEPTEMBER 1954

I flew to Malta on 13th April in an old and very shaky Dakota, arriving in Malta in the late afternoon. On the 15th, I was the CRASC Orderly Officer and on the 16th, I was on the rifle ranges for the annual Qualification tests. I was back in the army much quicker than I had expected. CRASC consisted of a Bakery unit, a Butchery unit, a Vehicle unit, a small sea-borne unit, a Cold storage and three Petrol depots. The HQ consisted of a Colonel, two Majors, two Captains, me and one Sergeant, two Corporals and a small number of military clerks and Maltese civilian clerks. Sporting facilities were very good. I quickly began to play lots of hockey and tennis and a little cricket - which was difficult to avoid. Inter-unit competitions were especially very popular. Swimming in Malta and the adjoining islands was almost perfection, the water being so clean and clear and the view below so beautiful and colourful. My work-load was very straightforward, no stress or panics. The duties of an Orderly Officer consisted of visiting the Cold Storage and the outlying Petrol Depots during the night and being on call in the office until 9.00am in the morning.

Sheleagh and the boys joined me within six weeks of my arrival in Malta and, as no official Married Quarters were available, I had to find civilian accommodation myself. After checking a considerable number of likely flats, I settled for one in Sliema, about a mile from Valetta. It was a new block of four flats, two at ground level and two above. I had selected one of the higher ones because of the better view and it had a balcony. It was quite spacious, clean and basically furnished with beds, table, chairs etc. It was about 100 yards from the Police Station and in the most selective area of Sliema. To my great relief Sheleagh was very pleased with it. Mess life was very good with lots of family entertainments. Schools for the boys, run by the Army, were first class and much superior to the ones in Aldershot. In August 1954, I was promoted to WO1 (SSM) and, as there was no establishment vacancy in Malta for a WO1, I was informed that I was to be transferred to GHQ FARELF (Far Easter Land Forces) in Singapore. Both Sheleagh and I were disappointed at having to leave Malta since I had expected to serve out my overseas tour of three years on the island. We had settled down very well, made lots of new friends and the boys were doing well with their education. It was a very good, healthy family Station. We left Malta on the 17th September 1954 on the Troopship 'Empire Trooper'.

Cricket Team; CRASC 32 Company. RASC Malta 1953. Winners knock-out competition. Fred Front row extreme left.

Malta 1953 (Cricket Final) CRASC 32 Company. v Gen HQ Malta.
Fred centre row on extreme right

CRASC Cricket Team Malta 53/54. Fred in back row.

Infant School Malta 53/54. Ian in second place.

St Andrews Barracks, Malta 53/54

Receiving winners trophy from the Colonel's wife.
Rifle Shooting

Malta 1953/54 RASC March Past
Fred on extreme right (Right of table)

The Empire 'Trooper'.

Built in Hamburg as the Cap Norte' in 1922. Captured in 1939 and renamed 'Empire Trooper'. Speed 15 Knots. Sheleagh, my three sons and I travelled on her from Malta to Port Said in 1954, where we joined the Asturius' for Singapore. She was broken up for salvage in 1955. I sa the Bell of the Trooper was in the Ministry of Transport, Berkeley Squar in 1960, when I was working in the War Office

HMT Empire Trooper; Malta to Port Said.

Sheleagh & Fred on HMT Empire Trooper. Sept '54, Malta to Port Said and transfer to HMT Asturias for Singapore.

Sheleagh and Boys. Transit Camp in Egypt, route from Malta to Singapore. Sept 1954

SINGAPORE

The 'Empire Trooper' took three days to reach Port Said, where we were due to embark on the 'Asturias' for Singapore. We were given very comfortable and spacious accommodation due to my new rank of WO1 and the dining arrangements were first class. But, I wondered, why wasn't the 'Empire Trooper' going all the way to Singapore? I had no duties, except for the daily 'Boat Stations'. The sea was quite calm, akin to a fish pond, perfect weather and my family happy and content. The boys were fascinated from morning to night with the ever present sea life, especially the flying fish and porpoises. We had three marvellous and relaxing days on the 'Trooper'. We duly docked in Port Said and, as the 'Asturias' had not yet arrived, we were accommodated in tents. To give us additional air-space the floors of the tents were three feet below ground level. We were woken in the early morning by a very tall Sudanese male with deep religious scars on his face and dressed in a long white shirt bringing us tea. An unusual awakening! On our second night in this tented area, a bomb was thrown into the compound which caused considerable confusion and noise, but no injuries.

We were quite pleased when the 'Asturias' arrived and we could leave the tents and go onboard where we were given a very comfortable family cabin. The 'Asturias', a much larger ship than the 'Trooper' had over 1,500 troops onboard, due to be disembarked in Egypt, Sudan, Aden, Singapore, Hong Kong, Korea and Japan. Our dining accommodation was very good with only one other family plus several wives due to join their husbands in Singapore, and six or seven senior WO's. The food was varied and sufficient and I had no duties to perform except 'Boat Stations' leaving me plenty of time to spend with my family. After about a week into the voyage I was asked if I would MC (Master of Ceremonies) the Inter-unit boxing competitions. I agreed to do it, for I would have been utterly ashamed of myself if I had said otherwise. I had attended many inter- unit boxing matches held in barracks in the past. I knew that this one, onboard a ship, would be much different. It was quite an experience to attempt to control some one thousand soldiers from about twenty different Regiments and all bawling their heads off. The Boxing went on for about four nights and although I enjoyed it, four nights was enough.

This was my fifth time through the Suez Canal to and from the Far East, Sheleagh Michael and Sidney's second and Ian's first. Michael and Sidney were only four and two years of age on their first trip, so they remembered very little of it. This trip was to be our longest and most enjoyable as a family travelling together. We had two very comfortable cabins with no undue restrictions, good entertainments, time to ourselves and no sea-sickness. Life was good. Movement through the narrow parts of the canal was restricted to a very steady speed to avoid damage to the banks. We were close enough to converse with the local people and the boys were very interested in the extremely heavily laden donkeys, lines of slow moving camels, flat roofed houses and the local dress and suggested that it was just like in the Bible. We were in the canal and its lakes for two or three days, the total length being only 100 miles, but there was considerable waiting time spent in the lake waiting to enter the next stretch of canal. Entering the Red Sea was a complete contrast with clear blue water and about 1,400 miles of it. The weather was fine and the sea was calm and once again the boys were fascinated with the sea life, especially the flying-fish and porpoises which flew and swam alongside the ship from sun-rise to sun-down. On the more sinister side however, there were the shadowy forms of sharks.

Soon after passing Aden, and entering the Arabian Sea, we spotted quite a number of large whales leisurely swimming together and totally unaffected by our presence. It was a long leg of about 1,000 miles from Aden to Colombo during which time we saw very little shipping and no land until we passed the Amindivi Islands as we neared the Cape. We anchored in Colombo (Ceylon) for two days for the replenishment of supplies and for the novelty of bartering and arguing with the Bumboat traders for their wares. It was quite a change to be stationary for two days but we were disappointed at not being allowed ashore. Our next leg of about 1,000 miles to Singapore in the Bay of Bengal was fairly uneventful; the Bay was quite calm with lots of marine life and the weather pleasantly warm. It took us about four days to reach Singapore and, although we had all enjoyed the journey immensely, it was a wonderful feeling to be on terra firma again. We had barely stepped on to the quay when someone shouted 'Kitna' (Urdu for Price). It was an old KOYLI friend, Sergeant Taylor, whom I had last seen in Lucknow Hospital in 1942 when he was on the DI list. He was now a WO1 in the Military Prison and Detention Centre in Singapore, as 2nd IC. Once I had settled in we reminisced over sharing bottles of illicitly obtained Port together in Mandalay and Maymyo in 1936/40; we also remembered the less pleasant times in 1941/2. I had barely managed to gather up all our baggage when another old family friend, T. A. Spackman, now a Lieutenant, turned up with the necessary transport to take us and the baggage to Nee Soon, a small military holding unit where we spent two days prior to married quarters being made available in Tanglin. It was like being welcomed home.

SINGAPORE 30TH SEPTEMBER 1954 TO 14TH JUNE 1956

After two days in Nee Soon, we took over a three bed-roomed married quarter in Tanglin, about two hundred yards from GHQ where I was due to work. It was the end house of a terrace, with a large garden. Fully furnished, roomy, cool and airy, Sheleagh and the boys liked it, which was a good omen. After we had unpacked, although it was mid-afternoon and quite hot, we decided to explore the surrounding area. The trees and bushes were so green, flowers so colourful and the sports fields so green and well maintained, it was such a vast contrast to the dull brown treeless rocky Malta. The barracks were only a short distance from our married quarters and seemed to have been recently modernised. We saw a well stocked NAAFI, an open air swimming pool, a tailor's shop, cinema, two churches and the WO's and sergeants Mess. We enjoyed the walk, well over an hour, but long enough for our first initiation to the sun and the humidity.

My appointment in GHQ was Superintendent Clerk of the Military Secretary's (MS) Branch. I had not expected this but one in the 'G', 'A' or 'Q' branch; MS was a small branch answerable to and with direct access to the C-in-C FARELF. The small but select staff consisted of a full Colonel from the Grenadier Guards, two Majors from the Dragoons, two Captains - one from the Gurkhas, myself, a WRAC Sergeant, two NSM's from the RASC, twelve Malay and Chinese vetted civilian clerks and one orderly. The basic function of the MS was the control of all Staff Officer Appointments in the Far East, their appointments, promotions and annual reports. Also the recommendation, notification and publication of all Honours and Awards.

For the first three months I worked hard and long late hours. I made a point of getting to know each one of my very mixed staff personally. They were good workers, always on time and very conscientious, which allowed me to settle down in my new appointment without any problems. Sheleagh quickly made new friends, enjoyed Mess life and with our first car, a Ford Consul, we enjoyed visiting the Island's varied and interesting features. The boys settled down into their new schools very well and we went to the cinema once a week. They also liked the sea and pond fishing facilities and voluntarily joined the local Church of England's Choir. Facilities for sport were very good, especially for hockey and tennis, and I played lots of both. In June 1955, I was awarded the MSM (Military Service Medal) by General Sir Charles Lowen, the C-in-C FARELF. Life was good.

On the darker side was the Emergency (war?) taking place in Malaya, just over the

Causeway, with the MRLA (Malayan Races Liberation Army). A total of 45,000 troops, 25,000 from Britain, 15,000 Gurkhas and several thousand West African were in Malaya during the so-called Emergency. After serving about eighteen months in Singapore, I applied to extend my overseas tour to three years. It was turned down because I had spent time in Malta. I and the family were very disappointed. In early May 1956 when we had been allocated a passage on the 'Empire Clyde', I was compulsorily extended for two months, Sheleagh and the boys making the voyage without me. I was extremely angry, especially regarding their cabin arrangements which were very badly and stupidly arranged. I was very close to getting myself into trouble. I left Singapore by air on 14th June 1956.

HMT Asturias. Fred & Boys, Sept '54.
On route to Singapore.

Our MQ Tanglin, Singapore 54/56

Fred and the 3 Boys. Jahore Bahru, Malaya 54/56

Fred & Ian Changi 54/56

Fred receiving MSM. The others received the LS & GC, May 1955

The Troopship 'Empire Clyde'.

Built in 1921 as the 'Cameronia'. Speed 16 Knots. Converted into a troopship in 1953 and renamed Empire Clyde. Sheleagh and my three sons came home from Singapore on her in 1956 - an uncomfortable journey. My overseas tour had been extended at the very last minute. She was decommissioned in 1957 and broken up in Wales.

Empire Clyde. Sheleagh and 3 sons came home on her in 1956

THE WAR OFFICE JUNE 1956 TO 24TH JANUARY 1962

A few days after arriving in the UK I reported to the War Office in Berkeley Square as required by my Posting Order. I was interviewed by a Colonel, the head of PA3, a Branch of the Adjutant General's Office. He wanted me to take up the appointment of Superintendent Clerk immediately, because of the Suez crisis and it's additional workload, also the appointment had been vacant for a month. I told him that I was entitled to, and had hoped to take at least twenty-one days leave, and the reason why I considered it should be granted. He was sympathetic and persuasive so, I settled for seven days leave and a promise that I would be given my full entitlement once the Suez Crisis was over. It was one of the best decisions I ever made. I now had seven days to find accommodation for my family and schools for my three sons. I was very fortunate to find a three bed-roomed flat in Tulse Hill, and still more fortunate to find two schools for my sons, also in Tulse Hill and all situated on the South Circular Road. Sheleagh was very pleased with the flat and after visiting the schools and meeting the Heads was very happy with the educational situation.

My first two days in PA3 was spent in attending talks and discussions informing me, and several other military personnel, how to adjust to procedures in an Office of State. I was bored with this for two whole days. For the next week or so, I went along with the present daily routine, observing and listening with considerable astonishment. The staff consisted of thirteen officers and eighteen clerks. Of the thirteen officers, five were military and eight were civilians, but seven of the civilians were ex high ranking retired military officers. Of the eighteen clerks, six were military. Definitely a mixed Staff, male and female, old and young.

PA3 was responsible for the Publication and Administration of Army Regulations, Manuals and Instructions in respect of Other Ranks (OR's). Their terms of Service, Promotion, Leave, Pay, Welfare and Discharge. On my last appointment in Singapore, my work had been solely in respect of officers - quite a change! My office was situated in Berkeley Square on the third floor; spacious, plenty of windows and a very good view. A blue plaque on one of the houses noted that, 'Clive of India' had lived there. The office in general was badly organised, very untidy and lax in security of correspondence and documents. The Manuals, Regulations etc, the backbone of the office, had not been kept up-to-date with amendments. It took me, using the military clerks only, at least two months to bring them up-to-date. My predecessor, a very sick man, had let the office seriously deteriorate. He was discharged on medical grounds a month prior to my arrival. I was in my office by 8.30am and was generally the last to leave at about 6.00pm, partly because of work, but also to avoid the London nightly stampede to get home. I couldn't believe that I was now in the War Office, the highest office in the Army. Any regulation or instruction I wished to see, or read, was now available to me. I was already security vetted for any document or correspondence up to and including 'Top Secret'. I had been in the KOYLI for over twelve years and had never seen any kind of Army Regulations. I made a special effort to get to know, without being too nosey, the civilian clerks, where they lived, their hobbies, likes and dislikes. On the whole they were, except for the odd one, a decent lot. I made no marked changes to the general running of the office for about six weeks. With the military clerks it was easy, but with the civilian clerks I had to be extremely careful, there being so many regulations governing their employment. They were, after all, civil servants who couldn't be sacked unless they committed murder; they had a guaranteed job until retirement. I worked closely with the officers and got on very well with them. I had taken the opportunity, on taking up my appointment, of checking their records in the Gradation List; the majority of them had served long periods in the Far East and that helped considerably. Not all the work in PA3 was dull and repetitive. We received lots of queries (Blue File Covers) from Members of Parliament regarding the Call-Up of men for National Service. Questions from Ministers (Green File Covers) such as, 'How many coloured soldiers were there in the army, by Regiment. Such questions were raised in Parliament and required a quick answer, often making a lot of work. We also had a daily two hour direct telephone line to GHQ, BAOR (British Army of the Rhine) in respect of Emergency Welfare cases. One of the many daily cases we received from SSAFA was in respect of a wife (Mrs Howie) who was about to have a serious heart operation. Her husband, Staff Sergeant Howie was in Germany; I knew them both well, Howie had been on my Office staff in Malta. I confirmed the necessary details with SSAFA and then rang General Head Quarters BAOR approving the immediate and urgent return of Howie to the UK on ten days compassionate leave. I went to see her in hospital after lunch and told her that Bob would be with her by night or early next morning. She was very surprised to see me and very pleased and relieved to hear of Bob's early arrival. She had already had the operation, plus further operation complications and looked extremely pale and frail. She was five feet tall, but looked like a child in a big bed. The operation was successful and we kept in touch for several years.

Although initially I did not like the idea of working in London, Sheleagh and I did take every opportunity in respect of the social life it offered. We visited all the main exhibitions, Flower Shows, Plays and Films, Football Clubs, Tower of London etc. I managed to obtain two seated tickets for the Trooping of the Colour in Horse Guards Parade and later a seat for Sheleagh at the wedding of Princess Margaret. I was appointed SSN (First Class) on 7th July 1959, RASC Corps Order twelve of 6th May 1959. One of the perks of the appointment was that if I was detailed to attend a parade, I take up a position as an Officer. After spending eighteen months in Tulse Hill we moved as a family into fully furnished married quarters in Bushey near Watford, a little further for me to travel to work and a change of schools for the boys, but a much better environment and more comfortable accommodation. I was awarded the MBE on the 10thJune 1961 (London Gazette Supplement of 10th June 1961). I was invested by the Queen with the medal at Buckingham Palace on the 18th October 1961. Sheleagh, Michael in naval uniform and Sidney attended the Investiture. We had lunch in Bond Street later. I was granted a Regular Army Commission on 25th January 1962 (London Gazette Supplement of 13th March 1962) and informed that I was to be posted to No 3 Supply Reserve Depot (SRD) in Taunton, Somerset. I quickly sent off a request to the WO Stationery Office for relevant Regulations and Pamphlets in respect of the organisation of SRD's. I wanted to improve my knowledge on SRD's prior to my joining for duty.

TAUNTON FEBRUARY 1962 TO OCTOBER 1965

I was given eleven days leave, during which I was fully occupied in preparing for my new appointment as a Regular Army Officer. I reported to the RASC Depot at Borden in Aldershot for commissioning documentation, posting details and final medical test. My rank was confirmed as Lieutenant, with three years seniority towards Captain. I spent several days at Moss Bros, of Covent Garden being measured up and kitted out for two suits of Khaki uniforms, Mess Dress, Great Coat plus masses of other necessary items, all at Government expense.

Sheleagh, Ian and I handed over 21 Ford Close, loaded up the Ford Consul with all our worldly possessions and headed west for Taunton. It was snowing but not too heavily. We arrived in Taunton about 4.00pm and were met by a Major from the depot (Masonic friend) and taken to our Married Quarters which was fully furnished and ready for immediate occupation. A most welcome fire in the lounge, a hot stove in the kitchen and a few basic groceries in the larder. I reported to the HQ Office early the next morning and had a long interview with the Commanding Officer, Lt Colonel Armstrong. He welcomed me to the unit and confirmed that my appointment would be Officer IC Supplies and Assistant to the 2 IC. I liked the assistant role since I would be able to see everything that went on in the Depot. He said that I should approach him personally if I encountered any problems in or outside the unit. He told me to concentrate on my work in the Depot for the first three months, that additional Regimental duties could come later, when I was settled down. The 2 IC took me on a Grand Tour of the Depot, which was very large, very busy and spaciously laid-out.

The Depot, situated on the outskirts of Taunton, and adjacent to the main rail line to the west, covered several hundred acres. It had a considerable number of very large storage sheds, each capable of holding several thousand tons of food supplies, and most with their own loading platforms. Other smaller sheds held disinfectants, water purification tablets, clarification blocks and poisons for vermin etc. The establishment consisted of one Lt Colonel, two Majors, two Lieutenants or Captains, six civilian officers, two chemists with laboratory and staff, about twelve clerks and accountants and up to sixty labourers, many classed as skilled. Attached was a squad of civilian uniformed police with an Inspector, two sergeants and several constables - male and female. The Depot also had a Customs and Excise House for spirits, cigarettes and tobacco.

One of the most welcome changes to my new career was that my work now started at

9.00am and ended about 5.00 pm. It was like working a half day - my married quarter being just three minutes walk from the Depot. My appointment in the Depot had previously been filled by an Officer who had been commissioned from Sandhurst, whereas I had been commissioned from the Ranks. A big difference. There was still a considerable amount of snobbery in the Army and I had seen it at its worst in Aldershot, the home of the British Army, where it continued even after death in respect of Memorials. I could feel it here with the 2 IC and the Officer I was relieving, but it didn't worry me in the least. I considered that I knew as much, or more, about the Army in general than either of them. I had worked in the highest offices in the Army in the UK and overseas and I had 30 years of service in the army. I was quite sure that I could and would acquire the knowledge and workings of the Depot. After all, it was only a great big grocery shop and I had been eating the stuff for 30 years.

I shared an office with the 2 IC and soon began to take over many of his smaller duties. He was not a very energetic person and was only too pleased to hand-over, especially any work which entailed travelling. Initially I spent a considerable time with the Depot's Accountants and their ledgers. This was a must as I had to be familiar with the procedures from start to finish. I was amazed by the amount of paperwork. I took my time and when I was satisfied, I transferred my attention to the large supply sheds where the bulk of the manual work of the Depot was carried out. Extremely large quantities of supplies were received daily by road from contractors, whilst at the same time similar amounts were being despatched by rail from the Depot to our regular customers; they being every Army and RAF unit in the UK, BAOR (British Army of the Rhine) and all British commands overseas. The total amount handled daily was enormous. We appeared to have the necessary equipment, transport, storage space and man-power as everything was going along quietly and efficiently. The depot was also responsible for the packing of Composite Ration Packs, one man, five men and ten men packs. The quantities contained in each type of pack were stipulated by the Chief Provisional Officer in the War Office. When packed, they were transported to Cardiff and stored in a Cold-Store, rented and run by the Depot. The total amount to be stored and maintained was the War Office's estimated amount that would be required to feed an Army for the first 14 days of war. Many of the packs contained items with a life expectancy of four to five years, which required them to be turned over and issued as part of the daily ration. One of the early duties passed over to me by the 2 IC was the regular check of the cold store. Sheleagh often came with me and spent the day in Cardiff shopping.

The days and weeks quickly passed by. I was always busy and often did a considerable amount of 'home work'. Sheleagh liked our married quarters, the best we had ever had. She also settled down marvellously to our new life-style. We had a weekly Sunday lunch in the Mess for wives and guests, which she thoroughly enjoyed. Every three months the ladies and guests were invited to the Regimental Dinner; she enjoyed dressing up on these occasions, which usually ended about mid-night. The 2 IC continued to pass more work over to me, but I didn't mind because the more he handed over the happier I was. I liked my work, it was a completely new experience to the office work that I had been doing for the past nine years. The more I learned about food, calories, germ organisms, packing, storage, life-span, etc, the more I realised how little I knew about it. As a sample from every contract coming into the Depot had to be confirmed and passed by the laboratory prior to the contract being paid, it was essential to work closely with the two analysts. I took over some of the additional Regimental duties, such as the Small Bore Rifle Club, Tennis Club and the Mess gardens, which were more of a pleasure than a duty. Sheleagh and I entered for the Singles and Doubles Tennis Competitions in the South West District and spent many enjoyable weekends and evenings playing and organising tennis.

I was promoted to Captain on the 4th February 1963. In April 1963 Colonel Armstrong was posted to a higher command.

I was very sorry to see him leave because he had helped me in many ways to settle in. The new CO, Colonel Hawkins took over command and made no major changes. In October 1963, the 2 IC retired and, as a replacement was not available, I was given the Acting rank and pay as Major. I now had direct contact with the Chief Provisional Officer in London. On many occasions I travelled up to London to attend Conferences regarding the packing, storing and issue of Composite Ration Packs. I held the appointment for about six months and thoroughly enjoyed carrying out the additional work and receiving the extra pay.

The 2nd IC, Major Bell, an ex Cavalry Officer arrived in March 1964. He bought a horse, stabled it in the Depot and joined the Taunton Hunt. Whenever he was away on duty, I fed and watered the horse, but declined to ride it. We shared an office and got on very well together. Work in the depot was running smoothly, social life in the Mess was very good, plus lots of tennis and Small Bore Rifle competitions. Life was good. In early 1965, when Colonel Hawkins retired, he gave me a good report. Everyone wished him well and we were sorry to see him leave. His relief was Lt Colonel Edwards, whom I met on his arrival in Taunton in the late afternoon and escorted him to the Mess where I had prepared the best and most comfortable room for him. I asked him if he would like some immediate refreshment, and at what time would he prefer to have dinner. He was extremely annoyed that the 2 IC, Major Bell, had not met him and asked me why? I made a quick and reasonable excuse. He was brusque and not at all polite, closer to rudeness. I asked him if there was anything else that I could be of assistance with, and was very glad to get away. Early next morning I informed Major Bell of my meeting with the CO; I never knew how their meeting went.

For the next few weeks there were many major changes, all on the direct orders of the CO with little or no consultation with his Officers. Systems that were working well and smoothly were suddenly changed for no apparent reason. He had not received orders from a higher command to economise on labour, storage space or to speed up the intake or output of supplies. It looked as if he just had a whim or fancy for change, and one of his quick changes did actually cause an accident. He ordered that pallet stacks should be increased by two additional pallets, which resulted in the whole of the stack collapsing. Three men were injured and two fork-lifts damaged; the bottom pallet had been crushed by the additional weight. On one occasion I was called into the CO's office to discuss some query regarding the movement by rail of supplies in the UK. After about ten minutes of one-sided discussion, he rudely indicated with a flick of his fingers that I should leave saying, 'We do not appear to be speaking the same language'. I later learned that he had said this to several other officers. The day-to-day general atmosphere in the depot was gradually going down hill. Social life in the Mess was deteriorating and where possible it was avoided. The coffee morning session was abnormally quiet and short. The Captain responsible for the care and maintenance of the Depot's Transport and Equipment was admitted into hospital suffering from a nervous breakdown and sometime after a more serious occurrence took place. The 2IC was in the CO's office discussing the daily routine of the Depot's work when their voices became much louder, more like an argument. I was extremely surprised because it sounded very serious indeed. After a few minutes silence the 2 IC stormed out of the CO's office, into our joint office, snatched up a piece of paper and wrote out his application for a Posting to anywhere in the world. Knocked at the CO's door, entered and placed his application on the CO's desk.

REORGANISATION, RASC TO RAOC

On the 15th July 1963, a reorganisation of duties between RAOC which resulted in all RASC Officers in the Depot being transferred to the Ordinance Corps (RAOC). In early August I was asked, on the phone, by the Chief Provisions Officer, if I would like to extend my appointment for another year. I gave him a very quick and definite 'No'. He was very surprised for he knew that I liked the work and that I had a son still at school in Taunton. He did not ask me why I had declined the offer, but I think he knew. One of my smaller duties was to prepare the Mess Accounts for despatch to District HQ. On this particular occasion I prepared them carefully and strictly in accordance with Regulations. The CO declined to sign them and indicated where and how they should be amended. I did as I was ordered and he signed them and off they went to District HQ. However, I did have a quiet word with the Superintendent Clerk of the Branch concerned who I had known for many years. A few days later the accounts were returned to the Depot, listing several required adjustments. I didn't mind doing them for the third time. I was posted from 3 SRD Taunton on the 9th October 1965. Michael was in the navy, Sidney had just completed his three year engagement in the Army and was preparing for

University and Ian was still at Boarding school.

Confidential Report - Taunton 1963/4

Captain Price is of average height, slim and he walks with a lively step. He has a calm temperament and alert manner. He expresses himself clearly, gives straightforward opinions in a tactful manner with the intention to address, and then accepts a decision without quibble.

He is a most loyal and hard worker, having the ability to deal with many subjects at a time without neglecting any of them.

In the period Nov 1963 to Mar 1964 when the post of 2 IC and Supplies Officer (Major) was unfilled, Captain Price carried out the duties of next higher rank (Major), and we worked closely together. I have been most impressed by his ability this year, his air of efficiency and grip of the situation creates confidence and respect.

In addition to management of the technical task he has continued to deal with Regimental duties with credit, including leadership of the Small Bore team, tennis, Mess Secretary and organisational issues. He has shown that he enjoys responsibility and the opportunity to control and I am glad that it has been possible to establish that, in my opinion, he has qualities which fit him for higher grade appointments in the QM field.

Signed; Hawkins, Lt Colonel Commanding, 3 Supply Reserve Depot.

RASC Barrack Officers Course 1963, Buller Barracks, Aldershot. Fred extreme right front row

Taunton 1964. Opening new Laboratory in 3SRD RASC Fred second from right

TO SINGAPORE BY RAF CHARTER, 9TH OCTOBER 1965

During a heavy rain storm we crash landed on the island of Gan, a small RAF Base in the middle of the Indian Ocean, The plane appeared to touch the sea prior to reaching hard ground with a very loud bump. It threw up large clumps of earth, clearly seen by the passengers. I remarked in a fairly loud voice, "not to worry, the RAF often land like this". I had barely finished speaking, when the plane, clearly out of control, tore down telephone and electrical wiring, bumping along for a few more yards and finally coming to a stop with its nose stuck in the ground and its tail high up in the air at a very steep angle. The fire engines were quickly on the spot and covered the plane with foam. The passengers were very noisy and scared, but there was no real panic. Those in the front of the plane made a fairly easy and quick exit, but for those high up in the tail it was a little more difficult. I told them that if they kept calm and stopped making a noise they would be alright and out within the next few minutes. A couple of paratroopers quickly released the emergency chute, slid down it and made it secure to the ground. It looked a long way to the ground. Initially several of the passengers required firm encouragement to get into the chute, but a warning of the likelihood of fire helped. As one person touched the ground another one was on the way. An elderly man, a civilian, the last of the passengers, was scared stiff. I had to literally lift him up and place him in the chute, place his arms to his side to avoid canvas burns and send him on his way. All safely out without any serious injuries. We spent the night on the island in ad hoc accommodation, men and women in separate areas. I was accommodated in a two bed-roomed hut with an RAF Officer who spent the night and the early morning in the bar of the Officers Mess. Unfortunately, I was robbed during the night. I had placed my pants, which contained my wallet, Bankers cheques and Identity Card under my pillow. They were taken whilst I slept. There were a number of Indians employed by the RAF on the island. I don't know whether I was lucky or unlucky - if I had woken up, I may not have lost my pants, but on the other hand, I may have got a heavy blow to the head. Either way, the fact was that we were now broke; I had nothing and Sheleagh had less than £1. I had to report the theft because of the loss of my Identity Card, but what was more embarrassing was the fact that I was the most senior military officer on the plane and the only one that had been robbed. A relief plane arrived from Singapore and we continued our journey late in the evening of the 10th. We were met by an Officer from the unit which I was due to join and taken to Cairnhill Guest house, an approved temporary accommodation for Officers until they could arrange for their own permanent accommodation. The first thing I noticed on entering was the sign saying that payment should be made in advance. A more pleasant surprise was a large bouquet of orchids on the bed, a 'welcome to Singapore' from Colonel and Mrs Renwick. The Colonel had been the Commandant of the Junior Leaders unit in Taunton, and Sheleagh had made some small hassocks for his Unit Church. A real uplift to Sheleagh's low spirits. My first commitment in the morning was to sort out my cash-flow position. I visited my bank, opened an account and arranged a loan of $S 3,000; the Manager suggested that I should take more when told of my accident, but I declined - I intended to approach the Army Paymaster for an advance of pay. I reported to my new unit and arranged for three days leave to enable me to find permanent civilian accommodation. The Guest house was quite comfortable but we didn't wish to stay there longer than was necessary. I managed to borrow $S 5,000 from an Army fund, interest free, payable back within three months - we were solvent! We bought a second hand car, a Renault Dauphine, a very temperamental French Lady. Officers in uniform were not expected to use Public transport. Sheleagh and I checked a considerable number of flats in and around Alexander, Medway, Holland Village and Tanglin. We eventually settled for a new built flat, adjacent to the Botanical Gardens and a small Private hospital on Holland Road. It was a second floor flat in a three storey block owned by Gloria Woo, sister to the Prime Minister Lee Kwan Yew. It was partly furnished, in a clean and well-to-do area, and within five minutes drive to my office. All the other flats in the block were occupied by military officers. My new unit was 'Barrack Services, Singapore' and my tour of duty for three years, my appointment being Assistant Barrack Officer. The establishment of the unit was for 1 Major, 2 Captains, 4 Civilian Officers and a total of about 100 personnel consisting of clerks, store-men, accountants plus skilled and unskilled labourers.

For my first eighteen months I was responsible for the furnishing and maintenance of 4,000 Married Quarters, plus a few hirings for very senior officers. I had been accommodated in Married Quarters in Colchester, Malta, Singapore, Aldershot, Bushey and Taunton, so I had a good idea as to what I was about to take over. A big change to dealing with bully beef, compo rations etc. My work was very time consuming and repetitive, but on occasions rewarding when dealing with immature young married couples. Also, a pleasure handing out bills for damages to pompous, self opinionated Majors, with whom I stuck rigidly to regulations. Sheleagh settled down very well, quickly making lots of new friends and enjoying tennis and badminton, often playing in the heat of the afternoon.

The RAOC had a Holiday Club on the island of Blaka Mati where all the facilities for water sports were available. I became, after a considerable number of spills, quite proficient at water skiing. Sheleagh stuck to the canoes and trips on the motor boats. We spent the majority of our week-ends on Blaka Mati. We also enjoyed eating out in the cool of the evening under the stars and palm trees, with live soft music at the many and varied open-air restaurants.

The second half of my appointment was spent on the Administration and Maintenance of barrack services to units, establishments, hospitals and schools. My first objective was to visit everyone in my units as quickly as possible. I wanted to see their accommodation, see and hear their problems, and to arrange a good liaison with Barrack Services. I noted that many units were not indenting for their full entitlement of Barrack stores, which I immediately adjusted. Within two months, I had visited every unit and arranged a good working relationship between unit and barracks, to the satisfaction of both. I also fixed a firm day, once a month, when each unit could visit the barrack store for their monthly requirement of stores, replacements, breakage etc. I got to know the units and personnel quite well and was often asked to stay for lunch. Work gradually became less worrying and I spent a little more time on leisure pursuits.

Sheleagh enjoyed going into Malaya where the beaches were less crowded, sandy and clean. We especially liked Seremban for the scenery and the accommodation, sometimes staying there for the night. We also arranged to spend a week in Penang, but at the very last minute (we were actually on the train) we had to cancel; Penang had been put out of bounds to all military. A 24 hour curfew had been declared because of religious riots. This was disappointing, but we intended to try again. We received lots of invitations from units to attend their many and varied celebration days and cocktail parties. The cocktail parties were very nice. They were normally held on a well groomed lawn surrounded with masses of beautiful scented flowers and Sheleagh loved them. Pretty, slim girls in Chinese and Malay dress served sandwiches, drinks, tit-bits and cigarettes accompanied by live soft music. A very big contrast was the annual Gurkha festival of Dashain which was held by the Gurkha Battalion on the island of Blaka Mati, The morning event of the festival, for males only, was the ritual killing of animals and birds by decapitation, which provided meat for the evening meal. The main event was the decapitation of a full grown bullock by one blow, using the Gurkha kukri. The kukri wielder was commended with a certificate by his Commanding Officer for his skill and prowess. It was unknown for a second blow to be necessary. Junior and young Gurkha soldiers polish off the small animals and birds, goats, chickens, pigeons etc, by decapitation. Blood from the carcasses was daubed on the serried lines of weapons, machineguns, rifles, which was a ritual blessing for success. The slaughter took place in the morning and was watched by males only. In the evening there was Gurkha dancing, singing and a well cooked supper. I was surprised when told that all the dancers were Regular soldiers. They were so lithesome and graceful, their masculinity hidden by a painted face. One of them had recently been awarded the 'Victoria Cross' for bravery in Borneo. Gurkha women were not permitted to dance in public, but Gurkha girls under the age of ten were permitted to do so and put on a marvellous exhibition of Gurkha dancing, singing and acting.

In October 1967 I was informed that I was to take up the appointment of Officer I/C Barracks, London and that I should be there by 12th January 1968. I was very disappointed and surprised; I had expected to complete a tour of three years in Singapore. One of my last jobs was to hand over to the Singapore Government, the island of Blaka Mati with all its stores, furnishings, equipment and accommodation. The financial and legal part of the agreement had already been settled by the Governments. Everything on the island had to be checked and confirmed prior to the Battalion, less a rear party, moving off the island. I informed the QM that all stores must be in their respective places, as per Barrack schedules in order to facilitate quick checking. I spent two days on the island with four of my accountants, prior to the handover, to ensure everything was ready. The Battalion had left it in a very clean condition. It took the best part of a week to complete the handover. There were three Officials in the Singapore Take-Over Party, all determined to check and count every article, no matter how small. Every light socket and bulb was carefully checked. I couldn't blame them after all they were buying the stuff, or had already paid for it. It was a great relief to hand over the keys of the Island and get their signatures, confirming a satisfactory hand-over. My four Barrack Accountants had worked hard and with great patience. The only item I took from the Island was the Union Flag.

Christmas 1967 seemed to arrive suddenly, perhaps because of the additional work with which I had been involved. Christmas in Singapore is a big occasion the whole city, plus all the ships in the harbour being lit up and beautifully decorated. Sheleagh and I spent nearly every evening, during Christmas and the New Year at some sort of entertainment. Dinners, Dances, Parties and Drinks, Quite hectic. We had made lots of new friends whilst in Singapore and so we had a lot of 'Goodbyes' too. On the 12th January we had lunch with our friends, the O'Leary's at their Quarters. I took about 3 or 4 leaves from their 'King Wah' plant (Cirrhus) for propagation in the UK. Because of the flooded road after a violent thunder storm, a 3 ton Pick up truck was necessary to take us to the airport. On the way an officer's wife had an extremely embarrassing time; her child of about two years of age would not leave the Ahma. The mother had great difficulty separating the child from the Ahma; lots of screaming and tears. There were a few murmured solutions to the problem by some of the very impatient soldiers on the truck. We left Singapore about 11.00pm on a RAF plane bound for the UK via Cyprus. We had a short break of about an hour in Cyprus, just long enough for a quick look around. I think nearly everyone bought themselves a large wicker basket of recently picked oranges. The RAF crew found room for them.

Although I had been annoyed and disgusted about my tour of duty in Singapore being cut short, I was still looking forward to my arrival in the UK. We had arranged to spend a few days with Sheleagh's sister Molly and husband Les at New Maiden until we took over the accommodation booked for us in Putney. A cold and wet arrival in the UK, snow actually delaying our landing at the RAF station. No problem with Customs and we quickly caught a train to London. It was very crowded and, because of our heavy baggage and oranges, we got some odd looks from the local passengers, but it was worse on the London Underground. The train to New Malden was much better, and it was a great relief to see Les, Sidney and Ann at the station to help with the luggage, which had to be unloaded on the rails because the luggage van had not reached the platform. It was very cold and, after staying for a few days with Molly and Les we moved into the accommodation which had been reserved for us in Putney. It was comfortable, warm and spacious, but it was a flat and we didn't like it. I told Sheleagh that as soon as I had taken over my appointment I would find something much better and in a nicer location.

Singapore 1967. Medway Park. Sheleagh and Fred

Singapore 1967 Garrison on Ord Org
Fred back row extreme right

THE FINAL CHALLENGE – THE LONDON DISTRICT

After taking my full entitlement of leave, which I insisted on taking, and spending about three weeks with my predecessor visiting units in my future domain, I took over the appointment of Officer I/C Barracks, London District on the 7th March 1968. These were the most important and busiest Barrack charge in the UK. The three weeks take-over had been spent mainly in visiting just the major and important units; it took me a further two months before I was able to visit all the units, establishments, Hospitals etc in the Charge. The Charge covered Greater London and extended to Mill Hill in the north, Woolwich and Dartford in the East, Windsor and Maidenhead in the west. The Brigade of Guards, the Life Guards, the Blues and Royals and the Kings Troop were the major units stationed in Barracks in the Charge, plus normal Service Units. Over 4,000 Married Quarters and 1,500 hirings were located in the Charge, some of the hirings being for very high ranking officers. I quickly realised that I was going to have a very busy future. I also understood why my predecessor, Major Gilman, was prematurely retiring on 'Family Grounds' so soon after qualifying for his Major's pension.

Initially I had considered that this appointment should have been filled by a senior Major or Lt Colonel. I was not due for consideration of promotion for another ten months. A Lt Colonel, due for appointment at the same time as myself, had fiddled the appointment of Officer In Charge Barracks, Northern Command, a cushy little Charge in York which I thought should have been offered to me. I had served for 36 years and to-date my nearest posting to my home county was London. Much later I realised that perhaps I had been selected because I still had four years to complete before retirement, which would give continuity to the major changes due to take place in London during the next four years.

My office was in Regent's Park Barracks, off Albany Street, fairly central and convenient and occupied by the RASC/RAOC. My office staff consisted of two military serving officers, two Civil servants EO's, and twelve Civil Service Clerical Officers, Clerical Assistants and Typists. My Barrack Staff consisted of Barrack Accountants, Storemen, Meter readers and Labourers. All except for the Labourers, were ex-service Regular Army personnel. Barrack Stores were two very large Barrack Stores at Woolwich and Greenford (Perivale) providing a monthly service requirement for every unit and Establishment in the Charge. Another twenty smaller stores, conveniently located, providing a daily service for married quarters. Within two months of taking up my Appointment, Sheleagh and I had moved out of the Flat in Putney and into a Married Quarter in Mill Hill in North London. A quiet, green and pleasant location, open country, tennis courts, golf clubs and good local shopping and only five minutes walk to the rail station. After familiarising myself with the route, I often travelled to my office by car; less than thirty minutes if I avoided the rush hour. I was generally in my office by 08.30am and rarely arrived home before 08.00pm. I spent very little time with my family and had no time at all for sport or recreation.

Life was extremely hectic for the first year or so and very time consuming. There were not enough hours in the day or days in the week; time flew. But I liked my work and I knew my job. Barrack schedules and Regulations are basically the same wherever troops are stationed, but the difference in London is that there are so many so-called Elite Regiments with connections to the Royal Family. I had to tread very carefully, and on some occasions had to bend the regulations. I was promoted to Major on the 4th February 1969 which raised my status a little. I met quite a number of very high ranking officers in connection with married quarters and hirings. On the whole I found them much easier to deal with than the lower ranking Regimental Commanding Officers. The Civil Service Officers in the Ministry of Works, with whom I had to deal because our work over lapped, were very helpful and obliging. I had several military units accommodated in Public and Crown property. I normally spent an hour or so in the office in the morning and then carried out my visits to Units and Stores up to about 4.00pm, finishing off the day in the office about 7.00pm. When visiting the main units (Elite) I wore uniform and used a staff car and driver and was often invited to stay for lunch. On one such occasion, in Chelsea Barracks (Guards), I was introduced to the Director of Music of the Royal School of Music at Kneller Hall, Lt Colonel Jaeger. We had served as Boy Bandsmen in the KOYLI in Tidworth in 1931 and had not met for 37 years. We had much to talk about, and too much, after lunch (3.00pm) Port Wine. No work accomplished. Fortunately, I had a staff car to take me back to Regents Park Barracks. Several months later, Sheleagh and I received an invitation from the Royal School of Music to attend a musical evening at Kneller Hall. On arrival we were given VIP reception, escorted to our VIP seats, Sheleagh was given a warm blanket as the evening was a little cool. Then some wonderful music, played by experts - the 1812 Overture by Tchaikovsky. The musical sounds of battle were augmented by live, but blank gun and rifle fire. Refreshments and drinks at the interval and finale made a most enjoyable evening.

My first two years or so as OIC Barracks passed very quickly with no real problems. I now had a very clear picture of the layout and extent of my charge and had established a good working relationship with units. I thought I could now, perhaps, relax a little and take it easy. However, it was wishful thinking. In late April 1970, additional work appeared from all directions - a new complex of thirty married quarters for Other Ranks was nearing completion at Whetstone, North London. It was imperative that I was ready to furnish them immediately on taking them over from the builders and then get the families moved in as quickly as possible. Security for married quarters outside a barrack area was a big problem.

Units of the Brigade of Guards began to change over their stations and duties from Ceremonial to Regimental, and vice versa.

The King's Troop, Royal Artillery, stationed in St John's Wood North London was making plans to move to Windsor. The Barracks, when vacated, would then be my responsibility until handed over for demolition. The Military Hospital at Woolwich was expected to be ready for occupation within the next two or three months, the old hospital was well overdue for demolition. On my first visit there I got a feeling that the ghost of Florence Nightingale was still wandering around. The Household Cavalry in Wellington Barracks was expecting to move into the new barracks at present being built in Hyde Park, Knightsbridge in late October or early November. They were expected to be the most modern, high tech and luxurious barracks in Europe. The architect was Sir

Basil Spence and his representative on site was a Mr Angel. I visited the site on several occasions whilst building was taking place. On one of these visits I casually said to Mr Angel that the view from the top of the tower must be wonderful. He said," Come along, I'll show you". We, with two workmen, went to the top of the tower block in a rickety workman's open cage on the outside of the tower. No seats of course, so I held on firmly to the side of the cage to ensure I didn't wobble. I had never liked heights and this one was high, in fact thirty two floors. I didn't look down and attempted to look casually unconcerned to my fellow passengers, but I was very glad and relieved when we reached the top. It was a fine and clear day and the view was truly magnificent. I was very relieved and pleased when back on Terra Firma.

The Whetstone project duly came along and, by switching my labour force about and authorising additional overtime pay to the barrack accountants, it was completed without any serious difficulties. I could authorise overtime pay up to a certain amount without applying for higher authority. The various moves of the Brigade of Guards went ahead smoothly and without any real problems. I decided to take it easy for the next two or three weeks and spend a little more time on pleasure pursuits. Sheleagh would come down to London in the afternoon to do some shopping and meet me at some pre-arranged rendezvous, have a quick meal and then on to the Theatre;

a late train back to Mill Hill or a walk to Regents Park Barracks to pick up my car. We did this on many occasions and saw some excellent Plays and Shows. My brother William and his wife Doris stayed with us in Mill Hill for a week. They especially enjoyed their visit to the Palladium theatre where Danny La Rue was appearing. I think they enjoyed their stay with us and we certainly enjoyed showing them around London.

In late August, I was told that the expected date for the Opening of the Knightsbridge Barracks would be late October. I obtained the following data from Mr Angel...

Tower Block;

a) 1st to 28th Floor ... 112 Married Quarters (Four per floor, 84 2 Bedroom and 28 3 Bedroom.
b) 2nd Floor............. RCMS Flat.
c) 30th Floor........... Box rooms.
d) 31st Floor........... 2 Squash Courts and Changing Rooms.
e) 32nd Floor.......... Squash Courts and Viewing Rooms.
f) Barracks, Messes, Accommodation etc, for 500 Troopers, their Officers and 273 Horses - mostly on levels 1 and 2.

I visited the site regularly, keeping in touch with the daily progress and familiarising myself with the overall plan. One morning I was very surprised to receive an invitation for lunch from the Commanding Officer of the

Grenadier Guards. He would also like to discuss with me a confidential matter after lunch. This was unusual and I was a little perturbed but had to accept of course, it being almost akin to an order. I had previously been invited to lunch at other Guard Units, but only from my opposite number, not from the Commanding Officer. I went to the lunch in Uniform and in a staff driven car. Before going into lunch the CO introduced me as his guest and I sat next to him at the table. I couldn't help noticing that I was the only Officer wearing a strip of medal ribbons. The CO was very interested in my early service in the Infantry, in India and Burma during the 30's and 40's. I suddenly realised, with somewhat of a shock, that the majority of the officers present had not been born at that time. I felt quite old! I had a very nice lunch and enjoyed the company and the conversation; the colonel was a perfect host. Now I was about to know why I had been invited. The Colonel told me that one of his senior NCO's had been selling large numbers of sheets and blankets to the 'black market' in London. He said it was a case that necessitated a Courts Martial, which he wanted to avoid if possible because of the bad publicity his unit would receive in the London Press. The items in question were, of course, issued by Barrack Services. I asked him why the loss had not been discovered much earlier, he said it was under current investigation. I suspected his senior NCO was perhaps his RQMS, a WO 2 and, therefore, this was much more serious. He was deeply worried and concerned about the publicity if the case went to a Courts Martial, could I suggest or help in anyway. After a very lengthy discussion and more coffee, I said that I would absorb the losses over the next four months by being more lenient on my Condemnation Boards and by the additional issue of rags to his unit for cleaning purposes. This to be solely between the Unit QM and myself. I said that the loss of a few rags should not be the cause of bringing dishonour to the Regiment. He was very relieved and said that the NCO in question would be very severely punished, hinting of a loss of rank, character and career. A few weeks later I charged the Guards Unit in Cavalry Barracks several hundreds of pounds for damages to OR's metal bedsteads, which I considered had not been caused by 'fair wear and tear'. They had been dropped from the first floor instead of using the steps. I could have added 'wilful damage' but I left that to the Unit.

In late September I was informed that the official date for the Opening of Knightsbridge was 22nd October. I had just over three weeks to furnish a large newly built Barracks, plus 15 Officers and 112 Other Ranks married quarters. The Officers Married Quarters were on level 2, the other ranks on levels 1-28. Construction of the Squash Courts, on levels 31 and 32 was still going on. I envisaged problems on my use of the lifts. I contacted the Civilian HQ that actually paid my Labourers, explaining the position, and got their agreement to my granting unlimited overtime pay, as and whenever I considered it necessary. I also said that I may require extra labour in addition to my own staff if the overtime did not suffice. They were very helpful and I made arrangements with the Ordnance Depot for an immediate delivery of eight loads (8 MQ's) for levels 1 and 2. I wanted to see how the three lifts coped. Time spent in unpacking, checking the contents, laying out the items in their respective rooms ready for the take over by the incoming occupant and getting rid of the massive amount of packaging. I put two Barrack Accountants and four Labourers on each floor of the four MQ's, as a best guess. It worked quite well, except for the availability of lifts. Construction work was still being carried out by the builders on the squash courts on Levels 31 and 32. I insisted on being given full use of two of the three Lifts, for the whole of every morning for the next 13 days. I would only need to use one lift for about one hour in the afternoon for the removal of packaging material. This was agreed. The speed of the Lifts was 500ft per minute.

The two Barrack Accountants and four Labourers, per floor, worked quite well, they needed very little supervision and welcomed the extra overtime. I arranged with the

Ordnance Depot for the immediate daily delivery of eight packs per day. I would have the whole 112 packs, whether unpacked or not, in the Tower block. With the furnishing of the Tower Block working satisfactorily I could now put all my efforts into the furnishing of the Barracks. I was on the site every day and all day, checking and keeping up-to-date with the construction. I could only commence furnishing when the Contractors had completed the construction of the building and the MOD had officially approved and taken it over. I was very impatient to get moving, but I did not have to wait more than a day or two. Building after building was quickly approved by the MOD and we were suddenly very busy. As a building was taken over, it was immediately furnished, checked by an Accountant, recorded, confirmed by the Regimental Representative and signed for. Furnishing was fairly uniform as every room, large or small, (eg a Dining room for 500 Troopers or a cell in a Guardroom) had its own listed requirement of Barrack Stores. I could also call-forward the stores from the Ordnance Depot as and when I required them. Although work was proceeding quite smoothly I was still a little more than concerned about completing the furnishing on time for the formal opening. To ensure it was done, I put in a request for additional labour of ten men for two days; I was given five men and five women. They were lazy, work shy, argumentative and disruptive. The very dregs of London's labour and a complete waste of time and money. I regretted putting in for the additional labour, but was glad that I asked or two days only. My own staff, Accountants, Store men and Labourers, nearly all ex Regular soldiers, worked hard, long hours and willingly for the next three weeks. Furnishing was completed on Monday 19th October. I left the site in the evening, relaxed for the first time for over three worrying weeks.

I received, which I had expected, an invitation for myself and Sheleagh to attend the opening of the Barracks on Thursday 22nd October, also a second invitation to attend a Ball in the evening. Sheleagh was spending the week in Wistow near Selby where we had recently bought a bungalow and decided to stay there rather than attend the Opening and the Ball. I couldn't query her, the bungalow was our first own home since marrying in 1941. I went to the Opening myself. The Household Cavalry Regiment led by Field Marshal Gerald Templar, Colonel of the Blues and Royals, and Field Marshal Admiral of the Fleet, Earl Mountbatten of Burma, Colonel of the Life Guards, rode from Wellington Barracks, where they had been stationed for five years. They halted at the Main Gate of the new Barracks, where the two Field Marshals dismounted and unveiled the Plaque commemorating this momentous occasion. This was followed by a short prayer by the Chaplain of the Household Division. I had a VIP seat directly opposite the Main Gate and had, therefore, a very close view of the whole procedure. Over 270 Mounted Troopers in full dress uniform riding immaculately groomed horses performed perfectly skilled drill movements. The Regiment, led by the two Field Marshals, rode through the Main Gate into their new Barracks at Knightsbridge, Hyde Park. Refreshments for Officers were served in the Gymnasium and it was here that I also heard the two Field Marshal's (FM) at close hand. I had seen FM Templer in Singapore in 1954, when he was C-in-C and High commissioner of Malaya, and FM Mountbatten in Burma in 1942/3. A very interesting and entertaining day, but also a day when I could now relax and leave Knightsbridge to settle in. I received several letters from HQ Ordnance, London District, congratulating me on completing the furnishing of Knightsbridge efficiently and on time. I now had just over one year to serve before my retirement, which I was determined to enjoy.

We bought the bungalow in Wistow, Selby for £3,000, two or three weeks prior to my Handing over the Hyde Park Barracks to the Household Cavalry. The bungalow had a large garden to the rear and my brother William, who lived in Wistow, had sent us all the details of the bungalow, confirming that it was situated in a very nice location in the village. We travelled up to Wistow to see it late one Friday where we saw the bungalow and the owner on the Saturday morning, the

Solicitor in the afternoon and agreed the purchase immediately. Sheleagh was ecstatic and 'over the moon' at having our very own home at last, having lived in Army accommodation for over thirty years and having lived in many different countries; over 27 different homes in unusual and often under difficult circumstances.

My brother William kept an eye on the bungalow for the first few weeks until we had the time to begin the furnishing. We began to travel regularly up to Wistow late on Fridays, in time for a Fish and Chip' supper. We selected and paid for the furnishings and arranged for them to be delivered on the following Saturday. This was repeated each week and it worked quite well. We travelled back to Mill Hill very late on the Sunday and I was always in my office in Regents Park by 8.30 am on Monday. I expected and looked forward to the handover of my duties to my successor in early November 1971. I was entitled to four weeks leave and also six weeks of Resettlement and Employment Training, which I intended to definitely take. My actual retirement date was 23rd February 1972, my 55th birthday.

My Superior's Annual Report on my work had sometimes stated that I should delegate more to my subordinates. I was determined that this would not be on my next and last report. In the latter part of my service I delegated all the routine office work to my civilian officers, all regular monthly visits to my two Military Officers, plus all minor queries and disputes. Any query, or dispute of any concern, to be immediately referred to me. I was determined that Sheleagh and I should take full advantage of the large and varied entertainment available in London during the last year of my Army Service. Sheleagh got quite accustomed to the rail journey from Mill Hill into London, where I would meet her and, after a little walk, some refreshment and on to whatever I had booked. We travelled back to Mill Hill in my car or by train. Sometimes quite late at night or early morning.

Every Friday, about 6.00pm, we went up to Random Stone in Wistow, it being very unusual to miss this weekly visit. On one of the occasions we missed, it was because we were invited by the CO. RAOC to watch the 'Trooping of the Colour' from his office in Horse Guards in comfort plus coffee and sherry; it would have been close to treason to decline the invitation. I had a slight suspicion that Sheleagh would have preferred the visit to Wistow, however, she did enjoy watching the Parade. Mona, my brother Sid's wife and a staunch Jehovah's Witness, stayed with us in Mill Hill for a few days; they were having a National Meeting at Wembley Stadium. I met Mona at King's Cross where thousands of Witnesses were arriving in special trains from all over the UK. I took Mona to Wembley early each morning before going to my office. We also took her to see the musical 'Oliver', which I don't think she enjoyed. She declined to stand up when the Anthem was played at the end of the show.

In 1971 Ian's girlfriend Unni came into our lives. She was working and living in the Norwegian Seamen's Centre in London. On two or three occasions I met them in London after work and went with them to the Cinema. She visited us in Mill Hill and often stayed for the weekend, occasionally going up to Wistow for a weekend. On one of the visits to Wistow, they announced their engagement. They were married in Selby Abbey on 20th August 1971.

There were a few hiccups, some expected and some not, during my last few months in the Army, but none of any real concern or worry. Life was good and the date of my retirement was smoothly drawing nearer. On my last Dinner Guest Night in Regents Park Barracks, Sheleagh decided that she would rather stay in Wistow, so Unni agreed to come as my guest. I was a little concerned that she would perhaps find it boring - too many 'Oldies'. I had no need to worry. Sitting next to Unni at the table, was a young RASC Norwegian Subaltern with two colleagues. Unni's table name-plate was 'Mrs U Price'. Once they knew she was not my wife but my daughter-in-law, conversation never stopped. Unni was completely at home enjoying their company and the dinner. The King's Troop, Royal Artillery, moved out of St John's Wood Barracks in November 1971 without any real problem. An extremely smart and well drilled unit when on Parade, but individually scruffy and careless in respect of accommodation and Barrack Stores and Equipment, especially individuals in Married Quarters. I had to raise some very hefty fines and bills for damages, losses and dirty married quarters. The empty Barracks was still on my Charge for several months, until handed over to the Ministry of Works for demolition. Although I had delegated the monthly visits of the minor units to my two military Captains, I still continued the visits to the major Units. Some, like the Brigade of Guards (five Regiments) and the Household Cavalry (two Regiments) required careful handling. I had, on the whole, a very good working relationship with these Units during my four years as OIC Barracks, and had been invited to stay for lunch on many occasions. I wanted to make sure that this working relationship continued up to my retirement.

I managed without any trouble to get approval for my four weeks Resettlement Course, DIY, Electronics, Plumbing, Painting etc, in Richmond, North Yorkshire in late November/December, which I enjoyed and which I later found very useful and beneficial. There were two Air-Vice Marshals with me on the same course. My Dining-Out night, pre Retirement, was at the London District Officers Mess in Hounslow on the 20th December. I took along, as my two Guests, my Brother-in-Law Major Les

Grout and a personal friend from the Ministry of Works, who had helped me on many occasions when I was dealing with Public Accommodation occupied by the Army. It was a good and enjoyable night, meeting many old friends, colleagues and well known Senior Officers.

My relief arrived to take over the Appointment on the 3rd January 1972. The next three weeks were very busy visiting all the major Units and establishments. Checking and confirming the Store Accounts, Equipment, Vehicles, Office Records and Financial Accounts. I wanted his confirmation and signature that everything was correct. We didn't visit the accommodation occupied by the Guards on duty in St James's Palace, Buckingham Palace, Windsor and the Tower of London and I suggested the visits should be arranged through and with the Unit representative (QM). A week or so before handing over, I invited all the Storemen, Accountants and Meter-Readers to drinks and tit-bits at a Public House on Albany Street, close to the Barrack entrance. They were and had been very willing and loyal workers; they were all ex-military service personnel. A few days earlier, I had arranged for sandwiches and cakes etc, for an Office Tea party.

I handed in my complete set of web equipment, which for some unknown reason I had retained for several years, to the QM in Regent's Park Barracks, an old friend of many years. He suggested that I should take a full set, latest issue, of winter underwear;

quite legal - my records showed that I had never been issued with them and I still had about six weeks of winter weather to serve. I handed over the Appointment on 25th January 1972 and commenced my 28 days leave on the 26th January. I was given a Terminal Grant of £4,925 and Retirement pay at the rate of £1,575 a year. My Army career of 40 years' service was at an end.

I had my last breakfast in the Army on the 26th January, said a few last-minute good-byes and quietly drove out of Regent's Park Barracks; the sentry closing the security gates behind me. I suddenly felt quite alone. I drove through the centre of London to Putney where I picked up Sheleagh, who had been staying with her sister for a few days, then on the road to Wistow and our new home. It was a cold day and it was snowing quite heavily, but our thoughts were elsewhere - the new life that lay ahead. As we sped north I began to realise that I was completely free from Military Law, Regulations and Discipline. The air even appeared to be fresher and cleaner and the Yorkshire accent welcoming and friendly. We arrived in Wistow in mid afternoon, after a very hazardous journey, to a very nice warm bungalow. Brother William had thoughtfully lit the fires.

==//==

Fred & Sheleagh (After 50 years) February 1991

GLOSSARY OF TERMS

WORD	PAGE	DEFINITION
Trully	5	Horse drawn flat bedded cart.
Gunny Sack	15	Inexpensive sack made of hessian.
Peggy Tub	17,20	Large washtub in which a Peggy is used, three pronged stick with lateral upper handle.
Scratting	15	Digging/Picking potatoes by hand following plough.
Midden	56	Dunghill, Cess pit or refuse heap for domestic waste.
Betel Nut	59	Kernal of betel palm, chewed like tobacco.
Tonga	60	Light horse-drawn two wheeled vehicle with canopy over carriage.
Punkah	65	Large cloth fan on a frame suspended from the ceiling and moved by pulling cords
Topee	67,71	Lightweight helmet shaped hat made of pith or cork.
Dhurrie	68	Thick flat woven rug/ carpet used as floor covering.
Dog & Stick	75	Route march
Mannlicher rifle	78	Type of bolt action rifle used 1903-1941.

Repiano Clarinet	95	Designating the Band player as non-leading.
Murghal	96,219	Muslim dynasty of Mongol origin, rulers of India 16th-19th century.
Maidams	92	Burial tumuli of aristocracy.
Deolali	228	Location of British army transit camp. To lose one's mind, derived from boredom felt at Deolali.
Phongyis	125	Yellow robed Buddhist priests
Toc H	126	International Christian movement, abbreviated from Talbot House; T being Signals spelling in British Army.
Maidan	135	South Asia open space, in or near town, used as a Parade ground or for Public events.
Enfilade	192	Volley of gunfire directed along a line from end to end.
Naiks	217,223	Military rank equivalent to Corporal in the Indian Army and British Indian Army.
Imprest Account	224	Form of accounting system where a fixed amount is held in reserve.
IOR's	224	Indian Other Ranks.
BOR's	225	British Other Ranks.

MRLA	292	Malayan Races Liberation Army.
Dashain	317	Religious Hindu and Nepali festival over 15 days; the most notable of festivals.
Serried	318	Rows standing/ positioned close together.
Cirrhus	319	Night flowering plant of the cactus family.

PHOTOGRAPHS

CHAPTER 1; FAMILY AND BOYHOOD 1917-31

IMAGE NO.	WRITTEN NOTE/REAR OF PHOTO.
1	Family photograph. FLP front with cat
2	Six youngest Price brothers, Sid, James, Albert, Thomas, Fred, David
3	Post card 1900/2 from FLP's Uncle William from Fatapur Sikri, India., to his sister Hannah
4	Post card from FLP's Aunt Zillah to her sister Hannah..."My dear Han, another boy came last Friday shall soon have plenty for a game team. What do you say." Refers to FLP birth on Friday 23rd February 1917

CHAPTER 2-4; ENLISTMENT AT 14YRS (KOYLI), POSTED TO INDIA 1931-1936

IMAGE NO.	WRITTEN NOTE/REAR OF PHOTO.
1931.1	FLP 4688132 KOYLI 1931. Xmas leave December 1931
1932.1	On the way to Bombay, India. 4th March 1932, HMT Nevasa
1932.2	Agra 1932. FLP (Bandboy) 4688132 KOYLI
1932.3	4688132 Boy FL PRICE 2nd KOYLI, Agra, India 1932
1932.5	Agra 1932-6 Water Well & Barrack Room
1932.6	Agra India 1932-6 Typical Barrack Block. (Seven of these Blocks accommodated the full Bn.
1932.7	Barrack Room Agra 1932. Air circulated by Punkhas

1932.8	1932 4 KOYLI soldiers on a 'Dog & Stick' in the Himalayas near Chaubattia, India
1932.9	Resting on Mountain road near Rannikhet (Pakistan) 1932
1932.95	North western Frontier, India 1932. Two soldiers and mules of 2nd KOYLI
1933.1	Chakrata India 1933. FLP 4th from Left,,Middle row L to R; Clark, Tidswell, Moulds, Menton, Farr, Kemp, Judd, Boot, Martin, FLP, Hall, Wishart
1933.2	2nd Bn KOYLI. On the road to Chakrata, India 1933
1933.3	Fatepur Sikri Camp near Agra. 2nd Bn KOYLI 1933-5
1933.4	Agra Railway Station 1933
1933.5	Chakrata (India) 1933-4. Dog & Stick 2nd KOYLI
1933.7	Agra 1933 Boys of HQ Company KOYLI. FLP head on left of pillar
1934.1	2nd Feb 1934. Agra - March Past - Viceroy (Lord Irwin). 2nd Bn KOYLI (Trooping the Colour). Gen Deeds (Col) also on parade
1934.2	Agra India 2nd Feb 1934. Viceroy's Plane on Agra landing ground. The Viceroy Lord Willingdon attended the Trooping of the colour at Agra (KOYLI) on 2nd Feb 1934. A rare occurrence for a Viceroy to do this. Lt. Gen. C.P. Deeds, Colonel of the REGT also attended. Jim, Sid and Fred Price on parade.
1934.3	The Viceroys Plane. 16 years later I met the pilot in Aldershot. 2 Feb 1934 Agra, India

CHAPTERS 5-10; INDIA, BURMA, WAR YEARS 1936-45

IMAGE NO.	WRITTEN NOTE/REAR OF PHOTO
1935.1	Agra India 1935. Fred with Pith Hat, David econd from right.
1936.1	Agra india 1936. Fred 1st on Left 2nd Row. David Last on Right 2nd Row.
1936.2	Four PRICES ; Sid, James, David, Fred. Maymyo, Burma 1936
1936.3	Band & Buglers. Changing of the Guard, Maymyo, Upper Burma 1936 Fred and David on parade
1936.4	Frederick Lloyd, Maymyo, Burma 1936. Lee Enfield rifle
1936.5	Goteik Viaduct Burma 1936
1936.6	Hockey team; Fred, Armstrong, Judd, Moulds and Barrow Book, Schofield, Ackland. Maymyo Burma 1936/7
1936.7	Mandalay 1936. Two typical Barrack Blocks
1936.8	My Barrack room in Maymyo, Burma 1936-7 and 1938-1940. Taken by B Vause in January '05
1936.9	On the road to Khangi from Maymyo, Burma 1936 or 1939. 39/45 miles
1936.95	Maymyo Burma 1936. Fred and David on parade
1936.96	Talamba;2nd Bn KOYLI moved from Calcutta to Rangoon on her in March 1936. Jim, Sid, David and Fred all on board. Later picture - 3 funnels on ship
1936.97	Typical building and transport in Maymyo 1936

1937.1	Hockey Team; Band 2nd KOYLI, Maymyo Burma. Fred Back row extreme Left, David Back row three from Left. The Band team won the Bn. 'Scissors Cup' nearly every year.
1938.1	Maymyo 1938/39. Bn. Buglers and Band
1938.2	Maymyo 1938 (Band 2 KOYLI). Church parade. BandMaster JCJ Martin.
1938.3	Maymyo 1938 (2nd KOYLI) Bn. Returning to Barracks from Church Parade. Officer Lt Vickers.
1938.4	Fred & David Maymyo 1938/39 Burma.
1938.5	Maymyo 1938 (2nd KOYLI). Mounted Colonel TB Butt, Capt Roberts (Adj) Clarinet L/Cpl F Price, Bandsman F Plowman.
1938.6	HMT Dilwara 1938 FLP India to UK
1939.1	David Allen, Frederick Lloyd Price. Maymyo, Upper Burma 1939
1939.2	'Fred serenading us'. Fred with Sax, Graham and David with Towels. Ashford in background. 1939 Maymyo Burma.
1939.3	L to R Bandsmen Graham, David and Fred
1941.1	Feb 10th 1941 - Marriage
1941.2	Botanical Gardens Maymyo 1936/4
1941.3	The River Sittang. Taken by B Vause January '05
1942.1	Fred & Sheleagh Price, Murree Hills, India 1942
1942.2	On the steps of Havelock, Lucknow. 1942. Sheleagh & Fred
1942.3	Upper Topa India 1942 (now Pakistan). David with Wendy, Fred with Michael. Hospital and convalescence
1944.1	Fred Price (on leave) Havelock Lines, Lucknow 1944.

CHAPTERS 11-12; POST WAR RASC, ALDERSHOT 1946-53

IMAGE NO.	WRITTEN NOTE/REAR OF PHOTO.
1946.1	Hockey Team - Officers & NCO's Wing RASC 1946/7; names on picture b/row; Sgt F Mahon, Sgt F Price, Maj T Modesta, Capt F Hunter, 2nd/Lt A Dann. f/row; BSM C Conway, Col J Mullington, Lt/Col E Hazelton (Capt), RSM C Rusell, Lt/Col J Rush, Maj J Kingsmill.
1947.1	Hockey Team - Training Battalion RASC; names on picture b/row; Maj W Bate, S/Sgt F Price, O/Cdt J Bruce, CQMS G Dean, 2nd/Lt A Dann, 2nd/Lt J Bartlett.Capt F Hunter, Lt/Col A MacDonald, Capt R Worth, Sgt F Mahon.
1947.2	Fred & Sheleagh, Aldershot 1947
1948.1	Fred two from left. Aldershot 1948
1948.2	Field training. Fred on left. Aldershot 1948.
1948.3	Hockey team; Officer's & NCO's Wing RASC, Aldershot 1948/9. Fred front row third from right
1948.4	Sgt's Mess, Aldershot 1948. Fred on left.
1948.5	RASC Hockey Club 1948/9 Season (names on picture) b/row; Sgt Grant, S/Sgt Price, SSM Thompson, O/Cdt Carruthers, Cpl Wellington, QSMI Beadle. f/row; Capt C Bullough, SSM Osborne, Capt T Podesta, Maj R Worth, Maj J Bate, SSM Wilson, BSM Mahon.
1948.6	Tidworth 1948. Jean, Ian, Joan, Sheleagh, Molly, Michael, Sid
1948.7	Aldershot '48. Sheleagh Fred.

1949.1	RASC Dance Aldershot 1949/50. Sheleagh & Fred
1950.1	Aldershot 1950. Michael, Sheleagh, Ian, Fred, Sidney.
1951.1	Sheleagh Tidworth 1951/52
1951.2	SQMS Fred Price, Aboukir Terrace, Aldershot 1951
1952.1	Fred Aldershot '52

CHAPTER 13; MALTA 1953-54

IMAGE NO.	WRITTEN NOTE/REAR OF PHOTO.
1953.1	Cricket Team; CRASC 32 Company. RASC Malta 1953. Winners knock-out competition. Fred Front row extreme left.
1953.2	Malta 1953 (Cricket Final) CRASC 32 Company. v Gen HQ Malta. Fred centre row on extreme right
1953.3	CRASC Cricket Team Malta 53/54. Fred in back row.
1953.4	Infant School Malta 53/54. Ian in second place.
1953.5	St Andrews Barracks, Malta 53/54
1953.6	Receiving winners trophy from the Colonel's wife. Rifle Shooting
1953.8	Malta 1953/54 RASC March Past Fred on extreme right (Right of table)
1954.1	HMT Empire Trooper; Malta to Port Said.
1954.2	Sheleagh & Fred on HMT Empire Trooper. Sept '54, Malta to Port Said and transfer to HMT Asturias for Singapore.
1954.4	Sheleagh and Boys. Transit Camp in Egypt, route from Malta to Singapore. Sept 1954

CHAPTERS 14-15; SINGAPORE 1954-56

IMAGE NO.	WRITTEN NOTE/REAR OF PHOTO.
1954.5	HMT Asturias. Fred & Boys, Sept '54. On route to Singapore.
1955.1	Our MQ Tanglin, Singapore 54/56
1955.2	Fred and the 3 Boys. Jahore Bahru, Malaya 54/56
1955.4	Fred & Ian Changi 54/56
1955.5	Fred receiving MSM. The others received the LS & GC, May 1955
1956.1	Empire Clyde. Sheleagh and 3 sons came home on her in 1956

CHAPTERS 16-18; WAR OFFICE, TAUNTON, RAOC 1956-64

IMAGE NO.	WRITTEN NOTE/REAR OF PHOTO.
1963.1	RASC Barrack Officers Course 1963, Buller Barracks, Aldershot. Fred extreme right front row
1964.1	Taunton 1964. Opening new Laboratory in 3SRD RASC Fred second from right

CHAPTER 19; SINGAPORE SECOND TOUR 1965-68

IMAGE NO.	WRITTEN NOTE/REAR OF PHOTO.
1967.2	Singapore 1967. Medway Park. Sheleagh and Fred
1967.4	Singapore 1967 Garrison on Ord Org Fred back row extreme right

AFTER CHAPTER 20

IMAGE NO.	WRITTEN NOTE/REAR OF PHOTO.
1991.1	Fred & Sheleagh (After 50 years) February 1991

CPSIA information can be obtained
at www.ICGtesting.com
Printed in the USA
LVHW070620280323
742728LV00014B/901/J

9 781839 754890